# The Language of New Media Design

'This textbook is really a road map for how research in new media should evolve. It offers such an overwhelming variety of examples, it is so clearly written, it is so stimulating in research topics. This book should be the base of MA courses all over the world.'

Jan Renkema, *Tilburg University, The Netherlands*

*The Language of New Media Design* is an innovative new textbook presenting methods on the design and analysis of a variety of non-linear texts, from websites to CD-Roms. Integrating theory and practice, the book explores a range of models for analyzing and constructing multimedia products. For each model the authors outline the theoretical background and demonstrate usage from students' coursework, commonly available websites and other multimedia products.

Assuming no prior knowledge, the book adopts an accessible approach to the subject which has been trialled and tested on MA students at the London College of Communication. Written by experienced authors, this textbook will be an invaluable resource for students and teachers of new media design, information technology, linguistics and semiotics.

**Radan Martinec** owns a new media research and consulting company IKONA Research and Consulting (rmartinec@IKONA.com), based in Arizona, USA.

**Theo van Leeuwen** is Professor of Media and Communication and Dean of the Faculty of Humanities and Social Sciences at the University of Technology, Sydney, Australia. He is the co-author of *Global Media Discourse* (Routledge, 2007, with David Machin) and *Reading Images* (2nd edition, Routledge, 2006, with Gunther Kress).

# The Language of New Media Design

Theory and practice

**Radan Martinec and
Theo van Leeuwen**

Routledge
Taylor & Francis Group

LONDON AND NEW YORK

First published 2009
by Routledge
2 Park Square, Milton Park, Abingdon, Oxon OX14 4RN

Simultaneously published in the USA and Canada
by Routledge
270 Madison Ave, New York, NY 10016

*Routledge is an imprint of the Taylor & Francis Group, an informa business*

© 2009 Radan Martinec and Theo van Leeuwen

Typeset in Bell Gothic by
Book Now Ltd, London
Printed and bound in Great Britain by
Antony Rowe, Chippenham, Wiltshire

*British Library Cataloguing in Publication Data*
A catalogue record for this book is available from the British Library

*Library of Congress Cataloging-in-Publication Data*
Martinec, Radan.
  The language of new media design: theory and practice/Radan Martinec
  and Theo van Leeuwen.
      p. cm.
    Includes bibliographical references and index.
  1. Mass media—Technological innovations. I. Van Leeuwen, Theo,
  1947– II. Title.
  P96.T42M358 2008
  302.23—dc22                                    2008003874

ISBN10: 0–415–37257–7 (hbk)
ISBN10: 0–415–37262–3 (pbk)

ISBN13: 978–0–415–37257–2 (hbk)
ISBN13: 978–0–415–37262–6 (pbk)

# Contents

# List of figures

# Preface

This book grew out of an MA course in new media production which we taught at the London College of Printing (now London College of Communication) between 1997 and 2005. The course was based on the premise that new media designers would need to develop and integrate two key attributes: the rigorous analytical skills needed to design complex non-linear information structures and the creative design skills needed to design functional and aesthetically pleasing interfaces. This resulted in the 'two translations' pedagogy on which this book is based. The first 'translation' was the translation of a linear text into a non-linear model. As we describe in the book, we gave our students factual texts taken from books on subjects such as medieval polyphony and Art Deco watches, and asked them to translate these into complex diagrams that would make their underlying conceptual structure visible. The second 'translation' then fleshed out these diagrams into new media products by 'translating' them in navigation structures and interfaces. The method as a whole therefore integrated the disciplines of design on the one hand, and of linguistic and semiotic analysis on the other, and we hope this book will be of use to students and teachers in both these communities.

The course was originally designed and taught by Theo. When he left the College in 1999, Radan, who for some years had been Theo's closest research associate at the College, took over and, in subsequent years, brought many refinements and new elements to the course, such as the idea of complex non-linear models presented in Chapter 3, the rules of the 'second translation' described in Chapter 4, the idea of strategies and the generic structure model described in Chapters 1 and 5, the interdisciplinary links with research paradigms such as artificial intelligence and marketing indicated in Chapter 1, as well as the method for analysing and redesigning existing websites, which is demonstrated in Chapter 6. We had kept in touch about this aspect of our work, and when Radan also left the College of Communication, to take up a post at Ohio Northern University, we felt that this work should somehow be preserved. As it turned out, this book represents only half of the course, as we used the same approach also in 'interactive story' exercises, asking our students to translate 'linear' short stories into non-linear narrative models such as flowcharts, and then to translate these into interactive stories. We hope to publish this work at a later stage.

In the end we wrote the book almost as a kind of report on the course, staying close to our practice as teachers, and to the *process* of working with our students on specific analytical and design tasks. The examples in the book are, for the most part, taken from the work of our students, giving the reader a look into the kitchen, or rather the multimedia studio, where we worked so intensively with our students. We therefore need, first of all, to thank our students, for whom we were, at times, hard task masters, but whose drive and creativity always inspired us. We also would like to thank the other members of the teaching team: Alan Sekers, who provided the design skills; Godfrey Lee and Rob White, who provided the students with technical assistance; and Sandra Gaudenzi and Ella Tallyn, who provided the industry and usability context. Then there are the teachers and research collaborators without whom we could not have written this book — among them Michael Halliday, Jim Martin, Gunther Kress and Mick O'Donnell deserve our special thanks. And finally we would like to thank our editor, Louisa Semlyen, for her faith in the project and her patience when we did not make the original deadline.

# Acknowledgements

Figure 2.3 Reproduced with permission of Ministero per I Beni e le Attività Culturali.
Figure 2.5 Reproduced with permission from Jakob Nielsen, Nielsen Norman Group.
Figure 2.11 Reproduced with permission of Microsoft Corporation.
Figure 2.14a Reproduced with permission from Museo Nacional del Prado, Madrid.
Figure 2.15a Reproduced with permission from Office for Official Publications of the European Communities.
Figure 2.15b Reproduced with permission of Microsoft Corporation.
Figure 2.16 From *An Illustrated Encyclopaedia of Traditional Symbols* by J.C. Cooper, © 1993 Thames & Hudson Ltd, London.
Figure 2.21 From Wignell *et al.* (1989) – Table 2, p. 362 – Elsevier.
Figure 2.22 Reproduced with permission from *Southwest*, 2nd edn, by R. Rachowiecki, © 1999 Lonely Planet Productions.
Figure 2.30 From O'Donnell, M. (2000) *Revista Canaria de Estudios Ingleses* (issue 40).
Figure 2.31 Reproduced with permission of LS Group.
Figure 4.6 Reproduced with permission of Microsoft Corporation.
Figure 4.8 Reproduced with permission of Ohio Northern University.
Figure 4.39 Reproduced with permission of Rough Guides [www.roughguides.com].
Figure 4.51 Reproduced with permission from Visual Thesaurus [www.visual thesaurus.com], © Thinkmap, All rights reserved.
Figure 4.52 Reproduced with permission from Jakob Nielsen, Nielsen Norman Group.
Figure 4.53 Reproduced with permission from Yahoo! Inc.

Giddens, A. (1996) *The Nation State and Violence*, reproduced with permission of Polity Press Ltd.
Harman, A. and W. Mellers (1980) *Man and his Music*, London, Barrie and Jenkins.
Nielsen/Fowley, *Designing Web Usability*, © 2000 Pearson Education, Inc. Reproduced by permission of Pearson Education, Inc.
Raulet, S. (1985) *Art Deco Jewelry*, New York, Rizzoli, used with permission from Rizzoli International Publications, Inc.
Wignell, P., S. Eggins and J.R. Martin (1989) 'The discourse of geography: ordering and explaining the experiential world', *Linguistics and Education* 1(4): 359–92.

Whilst every effort has been made to contact copyright holders of copyright material in this book, we have not always been successful. In the event of a copyright query please contact the publishers.

# 1 Introduction

## Language and new media design

Language is essentially a resource for communicating through speech or writing. It provides us with ways of patterning sound or letter forms that are associated with meanings. These patterns and their associations with specific meanings have developed over time, in part through trial and error and gradual habituation, in part through deliberate and systematic efforts to regularize and regulate them. As a result language has become an immensely rich resource that allows us to communicate a vast range of content and to do so in formats that can perform a vast range of communicative functions – informing us, entertaining us, lecturing us, persuading us, and much more.

The new media are our most recent resource for communication. They differ from language in three ways. They are multimodal, combining language with visual communication and sound. They are non-linear, combining spatial and temporal patterns. And they are new, lacking the long history and the many years of systematic thought that have made language what it is.

But fundamentally, and in their essence, they are, or should be, like language. Like language they are resources for communication that provide us with ways of patterning text and image that users can, or should be able to, associate with meanings. It stands to reason that new media designers might have something to learn from the study of language, that it might pay to approach new media with the long-established and tried and proven concepts and methods of linguistics.

The fundamental idea of this book is that new media are, or should be, structured by invisible underlying patterns that connect image, sound and text into meaningful wholes. We call these patterns 'non-linear models'. Non-linear models are semantic constructs that map out the relations between concepts in the semantic fields, or fields of meaning, that underlie new media products. Meaning itself is of course intangible. It needs to somehow be made concrete, perceivable by our senses. The way non-linear models meet the eye and ear of the user is through their realization, or translation, into navigation and layout patterns in the interface. These are the forms by means of which the meanings, i.e. the non-linear models, are accessed. What follows is that the more clearly and explicitly the non-linear models are translated into navigation and interface, the easier it is for the user to understand the non-linear semantics of new media products, and the more likely it is that the message will get across.

## Systemic linguistics

The linguistic model our thinking about new media takes inspiration from is systemic linguistics (e.g. Halliday 1994; Eggins 1994). Systemic linguistics describes language as a set of choices, extending from the most general to the most specific. These choices form the 'meaning potential' of (a) language. They are expressed as abstract features that specify among other things the processes and entities that make up the structure of the basic unit of language, which is the clause, or simple sentence. These entities and processes are then realized, or translated, by verbs and nouns and other such familiar grammatical categories. In the case of processes, for instance, the most general choice is that between 'narrative processes', which represent actions and events (for instance 'walking', 'speaking' and 'desiring'), and 'conceptual processes', which represent more or less permanent and unchanging 'states' (for instance 'having' and 'being'). As can be seen in Figure 1.1, each leads to more specific choices. Narrative processes, for instance, include 'material processes' (such as 'walking' or 'building'), 'verbal processes' (such as 'saying' or 'asking') and 'mental processes' (such as 'thinking' or 'fearing'). 'Conceptual processes' include 'having' and 'being'. Needless to say, such choices lead to further, even more specific choices, until we arrive at very specific actions such as 'walking', 'protesting', 'smelling', and so on. The same applies to 'entities', as also shown in Figure 1.1. Different kinds of processes combine with different kinds of entities. 'Mental processes', for instance, combine with two kinds of entity, a human one, the entity whose mental process it is (it may also be any other entity to which we ascribe similar mental processes as we do

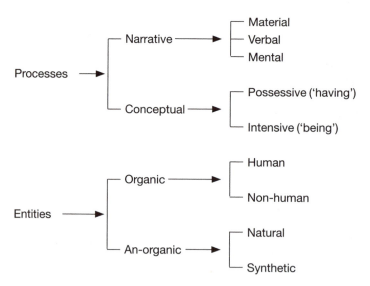

*Figure 1.1* Basic choices of process and entity

to humans) and the object of the mental process (what it is that is being thought or feared or whatever). For instance in the sentence 'He feared the worst', 'he' is what systemic linguists call the 'Senser' (the human entity who does the 'fearing'), 'feared' is the mental process, and 'the worst' is the object of the fear, the 'Phenomenon', as systemic linguists call it.

According to systemic linguists, language is always patterned to simultaneously communicate three broad types of meaning – ideational, interpersonal and textual. Linguistic messages such as sentences, and also larger stretches of text, always have an ideational, an interpersonal (we might also say, 'interactive') and a textual meaning. Ideational meanings communicate information, for instance the fact that there was a person who 'feared the worst'. But by varying the interpersonal patterning, different interactions can be created while keeping the information the same, for instance the choice between providing information ('He fears the worst') and requesting information ('Did he fear the worst?') (Figure 1.2). Textual meanings allow different parts of the information to be emphasized or foregrounded in different ways, and to create coherence and cohesion in longer texts. They do this both by cohesive devices that hold a text together – such as anaphoric pronouns that refer back to entities that were mentioned earlier – and by more or less rhythmically summarizing and expanding a text's content.

The linguistic choices of speakers and writers will be driven by their communicative purposes and by their target audiences. The same applies to new media designers. They also have different purposes to achieve and they must therefore also have different ideational, interpersonal and textual patterns to choose from. Internet designers refer to such communicative purposes as 'strategies' and subsume them under strategic web design; in systemic linguistics they have been referred to as 'genres'. Just as the linguistic choices of speakers or writers are attuned to the audiences they are addressing, so in new media the target audience must also be an important part of the picture. In our model of new media design, the characteristics of the target audience, which in systemic linguistics have been called 'coding orientations', have two functions – they provide motivation for the choice of one strategy over another and they influence the choice of translations of the meanings into forms, i.e. of the non-linear models into navigation and interface.

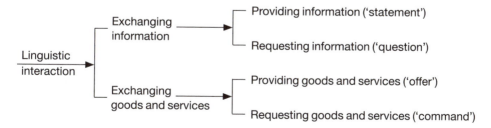

*Figure 1.2* Basic choices of interpersonal meaning (after Halliday 1994)

So we take six key elements from systemic-functional linguistics:

- Communication always involves ideational, interpersonal and textual meanings that run in parallel.
- There are systems of choices for all these aspects of meaning.
- These systems stipulate the available meanings as well as the ways in which they translate into visible or audible form.
- As shown in Figures 1.1 and 1.2, systems can be represented by what, below, we will refer to as classification trees.
- Linguistic choices are driven by communicative purposes, or genres.
- Different genres are ultimately motivated by different target audiences.

So our conception of the way new media work is based on the way language works, and indeed the way that other semiotic systems, such as gestures, images and music, work, too. At the same time, many of the concepts we will use have also been explored in related fields, such as artificial intelligence, cognitive science and visualization studies, and some of the ideas we use, such as the concept of strategy, are closely related to the way these terms are used in web design and in marketing. We will acknowledge this throughout the book.

## The thesaurus

Language consists both of grammar and vocabulary ('lexis'), and hence the language of new media design can also be seen from the perspective of the vocabulary. Roget's Thesaurus is a better metaphor than the dictionary for looking at new media design from this complementary perspective. A dictionary's organization is not based on the meanings of words, but on their alphabetical listing, which is semantically arbitrary. Our approach to new media design, on the other hand, is entirely based on semantic motivation – not only in the structuring of the content but also in interface design, and this has correspondences with how the thesaurus is organized.

Looking up an expression in the thesaurus involves something like the following. First you have an idea in your mind, a concept or meaning, for which you cannot find quite the right expression. So you look up the word that seems closest to expressing it in the thesaurus' alphabetical index. The first step is thus similar to looking up an expression in a dictionary. The index then refers you to a paragraph where the same expression is surrounded by other expressions related to it in meaning. One or more of these are likely to fit the original idea better than the word you first looked up. If it is still not the right one, the reference that follows it will lead you to another paragraph containing it and other, related expressions. Now you are likely to find a word that expresses your original idea better. If you are still not satisfied, there will be a reference taking you to yet another paragraph with yet other related expressions, and so on.

The semantic connections between these thesaurus paragraphs closely resemble the navigation links that connect topic areas in the content of new media products based on the semantically motivated design principles we will be proposing in this book. The paragraphs themselves are like the topics that fill the product's screens, and the process of looking up a suitable expression for one's idea in the thesaurus is like browsing through a semantically motivated website or encyclopaedia. At each successive stage (or click), some content related in meaning is displayed. Some parts of it are flagged, either by a letter–number combination (the thesaurus) or by underlining and similar methods (the new media), as leading to other topic areas, or semantic fields, which are related in content. The whole process in both cases is thus a movement through semantic space.

But this is not where the analogy ends. Apart from being organized in terms of paragraphs of semantically related terms, the thesaurus also has an overarching hierarchical, tree-like classification structure that starts with the most general and ends with the most specific categories. Its whole universe of knowledge is first divided into basic semantic categories: 'abstract relations', 'space', 'material world', 'intellect', 'volition' and 'sentient and moral powers'. Taking the volition path through the tree as an example, volition is further divided into 'individual volition' and 'inter-social volition'. And following individual volition in more detail leads to 'volition in general', 'prospective volition', 'voluntary action', 'antagonism' and 'results of action'. This general-to-specific structure is the same as that used by websites whose design successfully directs users to more and more specific topics of interest.

## Non-linear models

The general-to-specific tree structure, like the sets of choices used to define processes and entities in systemic-functional grammar, is based on one of the non-linear models for organizing information we will present in the following chapters, namely the classification tree. It is a common model, but there are others as well. We will describe the Given–New and Ideal–Real models, which are both based on the principle of polarizing, or contrasting, different kinds of information. We will also discuss the star structure, based on the semantic principle of centre and periphery, with a central, or nuclear, item of information surrounded by other items that all depend on it in some way. We will discuss the table, or matrix, structured around the semantic principle of comparison, where information items are compared in terms of some attributes. And finally, we will describe the network model, which consists of nodes and relations of many different kinds.

The non-linear ways of organizing information we have identified are truly semantic in nature. They have to be visualized somehow to make them concrete, but we do not draw tree, star, network and other kinds of diagrams unless they have particular semantic relations behind them. This is a major distinguishing point between our approach and the way information is structured in non-linear storyboards or 'wire frames' and, based on them, non-linear products in the new media industry. There, the division of content between screens is, as a rule, only intuitive, and the links are simply devices to indicate how the screens should physically be connected in the actual electronic product. The storyboard diagrams are referred to as 'trees' in industry parlance, and use the same form to represent a whole variety of semantic relations which, if analysed by following our method, are revealed behind them. The same is true of the products that are based on the storyboards.

It is, for example, common for websites to have a 'tree' navigation on the left of the web page, but often this 'tree' is not a classification tree, because it is not based on the semantic principle of classification from general to specific. It is not even a componential tree, which is a variety of the same overarching principle of inclusion, in which the semantic relations between nodes are of the 'part–whole' kind, but one in which the 'part–whole' tree structure is based on the physical principle of inclusion, following the structure of a book's table of contents, where chapters are part of the book, sections are part of chapters, etc.

Take the example of George Lakoff's book *Women, Fire and Dangerous Things: What Categories Reveal about the Mind* (1990). It has a table of contents with four levels. At the highest level is the whole table of contents. The second level is formed by 'Acknowledgements', 'Preface', 'Book 1', 'Book 2', 'Afterword', 'References', 'Name Index' and 'Subject Index'. At the third level, Book 1 is divided into 'Part 1' and 'Part 2', and Book 2 into 'Introduction', 'Anger', '*Over*' and '*There*-Constructions'. Part 1 and Part 2 are then divided into chapters. In the text itself, the chapters are divided into sections, which thus form another level of the hierarchy. The tree can be represented as in Figure 1.3.

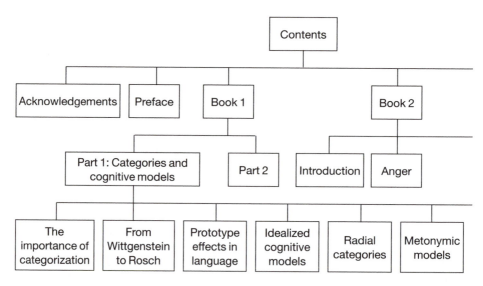

*Figure 1.3* Part–whole tree based on physical inclusion in Lakoff's *Women, Fire and Dangerous Things* (1990)

Like the table of contents of the Lonely Planet travel guide we will analyse in more detail in Chapter 2, only some of these relations are truly semantic part–whole relations. Due to the physical limitations of the book (an object which includes (the pages that make up) the chapters, which include (the pages that make up) the sections, etc.), the sections, chapters and the book as a whole are in a physical, progressively inclusive relationship. But the semantic relationship between the content that is in the sections and in the chapters in which the sections are included is generally not 'part–whole', but 'classification' or 'attribution', and other kinds as well. In the case of Lakoff's table of contents, Part 1 of the book is called 'Categories and cognitive models', and the chapters it consists of are titled 'The importance of categorization', 'From Wittgenstein to Rosch', 'Prototype effects in language', 'Idealized cognitive models', 'Metonymic models', 'Radial categories', etc. The content of these chapters is semantically related to the title of Part 1 ('Categories and cognitive models') in different ways. 'Idealized cognitive models', 'Metonymic models' and 'Radial categories' are *kinds of* 'categories and cognitive models', and 'The importance of categorization' and 'From Wittgenstein to Rosch' are their *attributes* (the former is about how important categories are, and the latter about Wittgenstein's, Rosch's and others' cognitive models). 'Prototype effects in language' are not even directly related to the idea of 'categories and cognitive models' but are the kind of 'fuzzy' categorization that is discussed in the preceding chapter ('From Wittgenstein to Rosch'). The semantic structure of Part 1 of the book is thus as in Figure 1.4 (the straight lines represent 'tree' and the slanting lines 'star' relations).

The new media are electronic, so they do not have the physical limitations of the book. It is not necessary to include topics, or chunks of content, in one large 'tree'. On the contrary, each semantic relationship can be expressed in a form that is proper to it. This potential of the new media for expressing different semantic relations by different forms has not been exploited, since many new media products still adopt the book metaphor and consequently the physical inclusion of all content in one large hierarchy. We argue that more local navigation systems, each with a particular form corresponding naturally to the semantic relations it translates, are the direction in which new media design should evolve. We also argue that, structured in this way, the non-linear semantics that underlies the navigation and content structure of new media products has a much better chance of being understood by the consumer. As in language, the forms should give a clue to the meanings that lie behind them.

A major distinguishing characteristic of our approach is that it is truly semantic – we only recognize forms that have particular meanings. We see meaning as primary, and form as secondary. This is true both of the way we visualize the non-linear models themselves, and of the way we translate them into navigation and interface. To give an example of the former, two of the non-linear constructs for organizing information we will present later in the book are the tree and the star. The tree looks quite similar to a real tree, although its form is of course much more abstract – it consists of a 'root' (the initial node), a 'trunk', which 'grows' out of the root, 'branches', which go

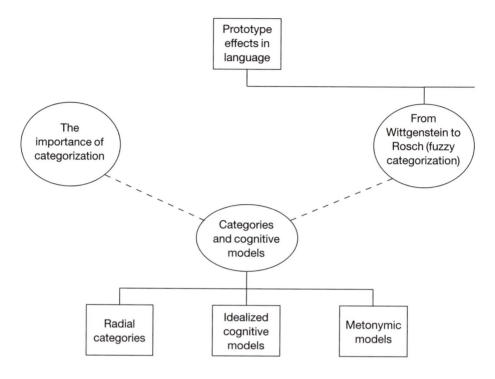

*Figure 1.4* Semantic structure of Part 1 of Lakoff's *Women, Fire and Dangerous Things* (1987)

off the trunk, and 'leaves', which are the nodes at the end of the branches. We usually represent the tree in the usual upside-down fashion, as in Figure 1.5.

The star also looks like the stars we know from our experience. It has a centre, or nucleus, from which rays emanate. The rays have satellites at the end, like some of the stars or planets do. This is represented in Figure 1.6.

In the case of the tree, the fundamental meaning is 'inclusion', and this can be of two kinds – classificatory (something is a *kind of* something else) or componential (something is a *part of* something else). In the former case, the relationship is of class and subclass or class and member. For example, MS Word is a kind of word-processing program, and Apple is a kind of company that makes computers. A computer, on the other hand, has a screen, a keyboard, etc. – the relationship is of a whole and its parts. The relationships that link the nucleus of a star with its satellites are different. Most often the satellites specify the characteristics, or attributes, of the nucleus or they define its identity. For example, the fox is said to represent slyness, cunning, hypocrisy, craftiness and guile (Cooper 1993). The fox is the nucleus of this description and the various attributes are the satellites that define its symbolic meaning.

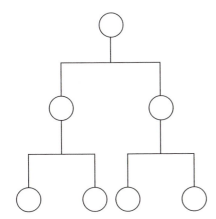

*Figure 1.5* Tree

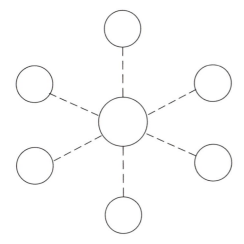

*Figure 1.6* Star

The star and tree relations are obviously not identical and, from a semantic or semiotic perspective, they have to be expressed by different forms. We will argue that new media products are, in their essence, semantic or semiotic products. In other words, they are products based on structures of meaning. As such, they could be considered kinds of texts, albeit non-linear and, much of the time, multimodal – we do not usually read or view them in a linear fashion, from the beginning to the end, but rather jump from one bit to another, and they tend to consist of images as well as text, and more and more often of video or animation clips as well.

Yet, we contend that this essential aspect of new media products has hardly been explored systematically to any extent, if at all. The usual information architecture approach, for example, often results in trees based on the old principle of physical inclusion pioneered by the book. This is perhaps not surprising, as the architecture metaphor derives from designing physical structures in the real world. There is no harm in adopting the real-world metaphor of physical objects in some cases such as the desktop metaphor that has proven so valuable in human–computer interaction, but in the case of semantic design, of designing relations between concepts or chunks of meaning, this kind of metaphor has severe limitations.

We aim to account for the fundamentals of the whole process of new media design, and we therefore divide it into two 'translation' cycles – (1) from a 'domain', or semantic field, to a non-linear, diagrammatic representation, and (2) from this non-linear representation to a new media product, with its screens and navigation links. The second step is in practice usually divided in two, with a non-linear storyboard being developed first and the product a close copy of it in electronic form.

Some of the non-linear representations, or non-linear models in this book have been used in cognitive science and artificial intelligence to model knowledge bases (e.g. Sowa 1983; O'Donnell 2000). There is also the related work on ontologies (e.g. Gomez-Perez and Benjamins 2002) and on the WordNet (e.g. Fellbaum 1998), and similar constructs have also been used to display information in visualization studies (e.g. Spence 2001; Tufte 1990). Our main inspiration, however, comes from systemic linguistics and social semiotics, where they have been used to represent lexicogram-matical structures (e.g. Halliday 1979; Martin 1991), the structure of texts (e.g. de Beaugrande 1980; Wignell *et al*. 1989), and different forms of layout (Kress and van Leeuwen 2007).

Apart from our approach being fully semantically based, our concern with the two translation cycles is perhaps its second most distinctive aspect. Non-linear diagrams have been used to structure information for quite some time. Interface design and visualization studies are more recent, having come into their own as part of the current new media age. Information architects have come the closest to what we are proposing; however, their information design being based on the *physical* world metaphor has serious shortcomings. We suggest that a chain of two *semantically* motivated 'translations' based on specific mappings between the semantics of a domain and a kind of non-linear model (first translation), and between the kind of non-linear model and the type of a navigation system and interface design (second translation) results in the best interactive products – that is, in products which are motivated both with respect to their content and their non-linear structure, and which express it in the clearest and most coherent way. As mentioned before, non-linear models combine to create larger wholes. Their selection is motivated by the designers' goals, or strategies, and their translation has to be appropriate to the target audience. In the barest possible way, the two translation cycles can, however, be represented as in Figure 1.7.

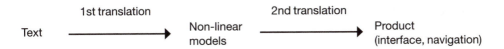

*Figure 1.7* The two translation cycles

## Strategies

We will now turn to the concept of goals, or strategies. In the design of new media products these are either developed by designers or by the managers of the companies or organizations they work for, or indeed by them both in collaboration. In web design they are the goals that organizations plan to achieve by means of their websites, often as part of wider strategies that encompass their other communications with their potential target audiences. Such goals can be of different kinds (Belch and Belch 2007) – companies and organizations can use their websites for purely communicative purposes or to actually sell goods or services, for instance. If communication is the only, or main, goal (the two goals are often combined), more specific strategies are then designed. A company may decide to use a website to provide a wide range of information, and some purely internet-based companies such as Yahoo! specialize in precisely that by creating portals to a variety of topic areas. Or a company may decide to do the opposite and provide information, or educate the user, about something particular, leading consumers by the hand, so to speak, and keeping them focused on a particular topic, which usually becomes more and more specific and involved as they make their way through the website. Companies offering information and consultancy about charity fundraising may, for example, choose to follow this strategy.

Some companies may want to use their websites to make an impression on their target audiences. Such websites tend to be targeted at audiences who care more about 'image' than about functionality. Clothing companies, such as FUBU (www.fubu.com) are a case in point. Other companies may simply decide to use their websites to generate interest in their product or brand, trying to make users stay on the site as long as possible by providing activities (e.g. playing games) and information about the brand, and by allowing them to purchase products related to the brand (e.g. download music tracks). The Pepsi website (www.pepsi.com) is one example. Still other companies focus on developing a relationship with their customers by providing forms for personal information and by linking the website with sponsored chat rooms and interest groups. This serves to provide customers with personalized offerings and makes it possible for the company to gather valuable feedback.

What is interesting from our point of view is that each of these strategies can be seen to motivate the choice of the website's non-linear structure. Different non-linear models, in other words, are suited to different goals, or strategies. The strategy of providing information on many different topics lends itself best to a network structure, which is a loose conglomerate of information topics or areas related by many different kinds of semantic relations. Companies wanting to educate consumers in depth about one particular topic tend to choose hierarchical tree structures that allow them to guide users into more and more detailed topic areas.

Companies that are out to impress are likely to make use of Flash introductions, which are often a purely linear element in their website structure. Since such intro-ductions consist of moving images, often accompanied by music or sound, they are suited to creating an 'image', and give the user enough time to take it in. Young, tech-nologically savvy audiences tend to like such introductions.

For companies seeking to generate interest in their brand, offering all kinds of activities and information on their websites, the network structure is appropriate. The same can be said for websites that link to chat rooms and interest groups, although here the network links are external.

Websites whose main, or only, strategy is making a sale tend to have very simple non-linear structures, guiding users directly to the shopping basket. With complex products, like indoor swimming pools, users are directed to promotional material, such as DVDs or videos, and provided with a telephone number to arrange a live demonstration. Endless Pools (www.endlesspools.com) are a good example of this kind of sales-driven website (Godin 2005), whose approach is 'get them in and get them out'.

Different strategies, or goals, thus result in differently structured websites. How-ever, although purpose may be the determining principle of a website's structure, the content itself has to be appropriately structured too. Different knowledge domains, or semantic fields, are structured differently, and lend themselves to be translated by different non-linear models and ultimately by differently structured websites. It may in fact be argued that the direction of determination is the other way around – that it is the kind of content, and its structure, that determines the website's purpose. In the indoor pool example above, the complexity of the product, i.e. of the main 'topic' or content of the website, determined its very simple non-linear structure. The charity fundraising website has a very focused, hierarchical structure because it focuses on one topic only, and because there is a lot to say about it at various levels of detail. Portals' purpose of providing information about many different topics is dependent on such topics existing in the first place, and on them being related in some kind of structure, however loose and varied the relationships may be.

Whether the strategy, or purpose, determines the structure of the website content, or whether it is the content that determines the website's purpose, thus seems to be rather difficult to decide, and may in the end be a moot point. We believe that content and strategy are, or should be, closely related. We will therefore be interweaving references to both throughout the book.

As for the target audience, we conceptualize it in terms of coding orientations (see Bernstein 1981; Martin 1992; Kress and van Leeuwen 2007), which are preferences for certain kinds of meaning on the part of groups of people characterized by various social and cognitive dimensions, such as social class, age, amount of knowledge or expertise about a domain, and aesthetic values. One of the effects of coding orientations is that they provide motivation for the selection of different genres or strategies. For example, organizations seeking to provide information about many different topic areas (e.g. Yahoo!) ultimately make that decision because they want to appeal to a very wide target audience. A charity organization setting out to teach how to construct effective fundraising websites presumes a target audience already interested in that topic. The other effect of coding orientations is on the choice of different kinds of translation of the non-linear models into navigation and interface. The various ways in which each non-linear model can be translated will be discussed in detail in Chapter 4. A non-linear model that is about a comparison of different kinds of watches, for example, can be translated quite straightforwardly, or overtly, as a table, which would be good enough as a reference guide for the target audience of experts who already know quite a lot about watchmaking. But a more engaging, covert translation, with images as well as text, may be seen as more appropriate by marketers seeking to entice an audience of women to buy the product.

## Structure of the book

This book is intended as a resource for both teaching and research that will hopefully be inspired by the integrated approach to new media design we are proposing. But it is also intended as a guide for practitioners who are interested in a new approach to non-linear, multimodal design of new media products. We will thus focus on the 'two-translations' processes, and will not be concerned with either the work of collecting information about domains (interviewing clients, observing their behaviour, etc.) or with user testing of interactive products' prototypes. There are various sources of information on both in publications on new product design (e.g. Cagan and Vogel 2000) and usability studies (e.g. Nielsen 2000; Norman 1990).

Because of the book's focus, as well as for pedagogical reasons, we have opted for using natural language texts as an input into the first translation process. The texts represent specific types of semantic domain which, because of their semantic structures, lend themselves to being translated by specific non-linear models. However, there is often more than one possible solution to the translation problem. In that case we choose the non-linear model that accounts for most of the information, or semantic structuring, of the text. The intention of the text, as realized by its lexical and grammatical patterns, needs to be respected when translating it into a non-linear model. Domains (and texts) of any complexity tend to require more than one simple non-linear model to map out their semantic structure. Such complex non-linear models consist of several simple ones linked together.

We have so far referred to interactive products as the final outcome of the two translation processes and this of course invites the question of what kinds of new media technologies should be used to implement the final design. Our students often used Flash and HTML, and these lend themselves well to one-off pieces for artistically inclined designers. But there are of course other possibilities as well. For large websites or information systems that need to regularly update content, the text and images used in the second translation can be stored in databases and accessed and displayed by non-linear models-based templates (see Veen 2001). But the design that is the topic of this book is in principle independent of any particular software that implements it.

The second chapter outlines the different types of simple non-linear models that form the basic building blocks of new media design. The third chapter deals with complex non-linear models, which consist of a combination of several simple ones. Except for the simplest examples, any new media products and any domains or texts necessitate complex non-linear models to represent their non-linear semantics. In the fourth chapter we present a system of choices for translating non-linear models into navigation and interface and discuss the motivations for choosing one option rather than another. The fifth chapter deals with the sequencing of simple non-linear models that make up a complex model when translating the model into navigation and inter-face. Finally, the sixth chapter presents two case studies, where we apply our model of new media design to analysing two existing websites and redesign them following our first and second translation rules.

# 2 Simple non-linear models

The simple non-linear models we present in this chapter form the basic building blocks of our approach to new media design. They are diagrams that can be used to map out the conceptual structure of texts or domains and that make explicit how such texts or domains are generally understood. Non-linear models underlie the construction of new media products. Taking this premise to its logical conclusion means that semantically well-structured new media products (i.e. products that follow our semantically motivated approach to new media design) make explicit the semantic relations between the concepts we build in our minds when attempting to understand texts or domains of different kinds. Therefore such new media products should make it easier to understand this semantics.

## Given and New

The Given and New model divides information into two halves, or 'poles', which contrast with each other in one way or another. A text contrasting the past with the present is based on this principle, as is a text contrasting environmentally friendly with environmentally unfriendly practices. In such texts one half of the information will be Given (e.g. the past), the other half New (e.g. the present or the future). Given information is presented as though it is already known to the audience, and therefore unproblematic. New information is presented as though it is not yet known to the audience, and therefore in need of their attention, and potentially problematic. In a text contrasting environmentally friendly with environmentally unfriendly practices, either type of practice may be Given or New. This means that Given and New can be manipulated to suit specific communicative purposes and audiences. A text in which environmentally friendly practices are New addresses its audience as if it is not aware of the problems that threaten the environment and therefore needs to learn about environmentally friendly practices. A text in which environmentally unfriendly practices are New addresses its audience as if it is already engaged in environmentally friendly practices and draws their attention to environmentally unfriendly practices (e.g. in China) that should worry them.

Given and New can be visualized by dividing a space (e.g. a screen) vertically in two halves, with the given elements on the left, and the new elements on the right, as in Figure 2.1.

Given and New is an information structure that originally derives from language (e.g. Halliday 1994), where it is realized by intonation. The melody of speech consists of tone units, or tone groups, each one of which has a main tone, or pitch movement.

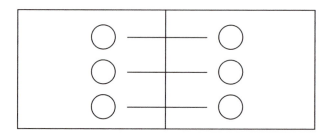

*Figure 2.1*    Given and New

This tone movement is usually placed on the word with which the new information begins. Whatever precedes the main tone movement in a tone group tends to be given, or known, from the context. Given is therefore what comes first, and New what comes last in the tone unit. The principle seems to operate in images as well, as Kress and van Leeuwen (2007) have shown, but there it is realized by the contrast between left and right. European languages are written from left to right, and this seems to create a powerful conditioning, according to which what is on the left of the written clause or sentence tends to be Given and what is on the right New. Many images seem designed to be read in the same way. This is most obvious in cartoons, as can be seen in Figure 2.2.

In this cartoon, Death is New with respect to Dogbert because it is the first time it appears. It is Given with respect to Dilbert because at that point it is already known from the immediately preceding context.

Many other images also use this structure. *Et in Arcadia Ego* ('I exist even in Arcadia'), shown in Figure 2.3, is a seventeenth-century example of the 'Memento Mori' ('remember you are mortal') motif that has inspired so many works of art – and Death, the problem at issue, is placed on the right, as the New.

Web pages often have the site's main navigation structure on the left, as Given, and links to additional information or to other sites on the right, as New. Arrows that lead to other pages tend to be on the right, too. As for the links themselves, the information that describes them is Given with respect to the information the links lead to, which is New. The issue of how much information to put in link descriptions (anchors) is an important part of web design. The more the users are led by the hand, the more information they are likely to be given about what is on the other side of the link, and the less 'New' the other side will therefore be. A good design provides enough information for users not to waste their time following links that lead to information they are not interested in. Figure 2.4 shows a web page in which the links on the right follow the Given–New principle.

Given and New is a powerful design principle for structuring the content of web pages. Figure 2.5 shows a screenshot of the home page of the usability expert Jakob Nielsen.

*Figure 2.2*  Dilbert and Dogbert (Adams 1995)

*Figure 2.3*  *Et in Arcadia Ego* (Guercino, 1621–23)

Figure 2.4  Hitdonate.net page (http://mysite.wanadoo-members.co.uk/hitdonate)

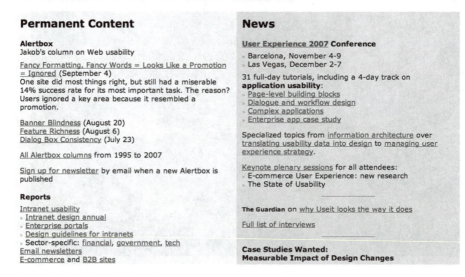

Figure 2.5  Jakob Nielsen's home page (www.useit.com)

The 'theatre analogy' text excerpt below is for the most part structured by the Given–New principle. Its non-linear analysis is presented in Figure 2.6.

> Ultimately, users visit your website for its content. Everything else is just the backdrop. The design is there to allow people access to the content. The old analogy is somebody who goes to see a theater performance: When they leave the theater, you want them to be discussing how great the play was and not how great the costumes were.
>
> (Nielsen 2000)

The 'photography analogy' text excerpt below is slightly more complex. Its analysis is given in Figure 2.7.

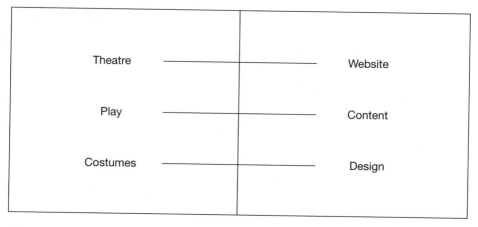

*Figure 2.6*  Non-linear analysis of 'theatre analogy' text

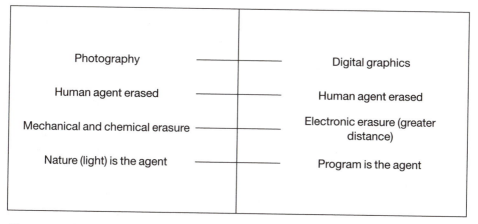

*Figure 2.7*  Non-linear analysis of 'photography analogy' text

The fact that digital graphics is automatic suggests an affinity to photography. In both cases, the human agent is erased, although the techniques of erasure are rather different. With photography, the automatic process is mechanical and chemical. The shutter opens, and light streams in through the lens and is focused on a chemical film. The process of recording itself is holistic, with no clearly defined parts or steps. For this reason, many in the nineteenth century could regard light or nature itself as the painter. Talbot did so in his book *The Pencil of Nature* (1969), and Niépce did as well, when he wrote that 'the Daguerrotype is not merely an instrument which serves to draw Nature; on the contrary it is a chemical and physical process which gives her the power to reproduce itself' (Trachtenberg 1980: 13; see also Jussim 1983: 50). In digital graphics, however, it is not easy to regard the program as a natural product, except in the sense that nature steers the electrons inside the computer chips. Digital graphic images are the work of humans, whose agency, however, is often deferred so far from the act of drawing that it seems to disappear. This deferral is especially important in real-time animation and virtual reality, where the computer is drawing ten or twenty frames per second, all without the programmer's intervention. The automatic or deferred quality of computer programming promotes in the viewer a sense of immediate contact with the image.

(Bolter and Grusin 2000)

## Ideal and Real

Like the Given and New model, the Ideal and Real model is based on polarization and divides information into two contrasting halves, or poles. But the meanings and forms of the two kinds of polarization are different (cf. Kress and van Leeuwen 2007). The Ideal–Real pattern divides information into the more general, or idealized, essence of the information (Ideal), and complementary details, or documentary evidence, or down-to-earth practical realities (Real).

Ideal and Real are visualized by dividing a space in two halves horizontally, as shown in Figure 2.8.

Ideal and Real have been used in paintings for centuries. Religious images especially, in their visions of heaven and hell, or of saintliness and earthliness, are most often polarized according to the Ideal–Real principle. Giorgione's (1505) *Madonna with Child, St Francis and St George* in Figure 2.9 is a good example of the Ideal–Real structure.

The priest and the knight, powerful symbols of religious power and earthly protection as they are, take up position in the bottom half of the painting, and the saintly Madonna with her even more spiritually elevated child sit on a throne in the top half.

Advertising has exploited the Ideal–Real principle frequently and to a great effect. Its function of selling often rather mundane products on the basis of exaggerated promises lends itself well to designing marketing communications structured along the lines of the Ideal and Real (see Figure 2.10).

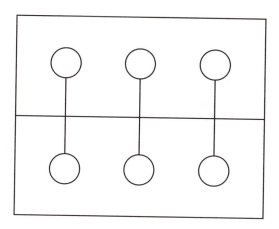

*Figure 2.8* Ideal and Real

*Figure 2.9 Madonna with Child, St Francis and St George* (Giorgione, 1505)

The broadband world is waiting for you.

In the broadband world, no one is an island. Boatloads of information swiftly move across the globe. High-bandwidth connections are seamless. Integrated voice, video and Internet/data solutions are cost-effective. Desk chairs can turn into beach chairs.

And you can turn to ADC. We're the global leader in innovative broadband networks and applications helping to provide unlimited access to information anytime, anywhere — redefining the way you live, work and play.

For more information about ADC call us at +1-612-938-8080 from outside the U.S. or 1-800-366-3891 in the U.S. or Canada. Or visit us on the web at www.adc.com/broadbandworld from any remote corner of the world. We'll be waiting for you.

▶ EQUIPMENT
▶ SOFTWARE
▶ SERVICES

ADC
The Broadband Company

*Figure 2.10* ADC advertisement (*Wired,* October 2000)

The rather exaggerated vision, certainly in the year 2000, of the new world of broadband wireless networking presents the advertiser's promise in the top half of the ad, whereas the bottom half contains more earthly and real technical details and other practical information.

Web design often follows the Ideal–Real principle. The company logo is usually found in the top-left corner of the web page, indicating the importance of the company's image and its elevated status in the mind of the company's executives, and consequently designers. The logo's positioning quite appropriately combines the Ideal with the Given, rendering the company's image as both full of promise and at the same time already known and unproblematic, 'given'.

If the content of a web page is expressed in both image and text and the Ideal–Real pattern is used, the images are usually in the top half and the text in the bottom half of the page. This makes sense since images, because of their iconic resemblance to the perceptions of our experience, are better suited to making an impression. They are therefore more effective at expressing a promise than text. Text, on the other hand, is better suited to spelling out details or presenting a convincing argument.

The Ideal–Real principle does not just apply to the positioning of logos and images versus text. Task buttons themselves are also affected by it. As the encyclopaedia screen in Figure 2.11 shows, major navigation buttons in CD-ROMs tend to be at the top of the page, while more utilitarian, or subsidiary, task buttons (e.g. printing, zooming in and out) are located at the bottom.

The text excerpt in Figure 2.12 is an exception to the rule that images are usually 'Ideal'. Here the text ('fan the paper') describes the action in general terms, while the images portray it in much greater detail and therefore have greater practical value as a piece of instruction.

The text below is from *The Cambridge Encyclopedia of Language* (Crystal 1997: 400). The upper part of the text is the Ideal. It in fact presents a general classification of definitions of language that could be represented as a classification tree (see below). The lower part of the text, in smaller font, is the Real, providing documentary evidence in the form of actual definitions.

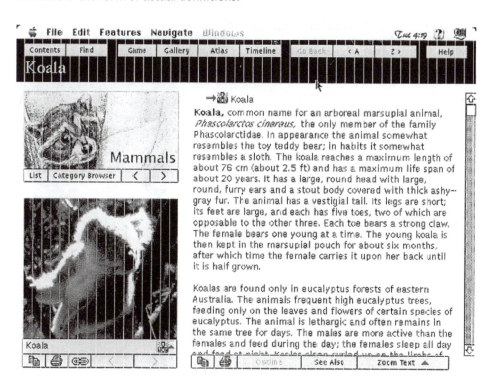

*Figure 2.11* Koala page from *Encarta* (Microsoft, 1994)

A widely recognized problem with the term 'language' is the great range of its application. This word has prompted innumerable definitions. Some focus on the general concept of 'language', some on the more specific notion of 'a language'. Some draw attention to the formal features of phonology (or graphology), grammar and semantics. Some emphasize the range of functions that language performs. Some stress the differences between language and other forms of human, animal, or machine communication. Some point to the similarities. ( . . . )

LANGUAGE DEFINITIONS

'Language is a purely human and non-instinctive method of communicating ideas, emotions and desires by means of voluntarily produced symbols' (E. Sapir 1921).

'A language is a system of arbitrary vocal symbols by means of which the members of a society interact in terms of their total culture' (G. Trager 1949).

A language is 'a set (finite or infinite) of sentences, each finite in length and constructed out of a finite set of elements' (A.N. Chomsky 1957).

Language is 'the institution whereby humans communicate and interact with each other by means of habitually used oral-auditory arbitrary symbols' (R.A. Hall 1964).

(Crystal 1997: 400)

## The star (Nucleus–Satellites, Centre–Periphery)

The star pattern has a central element and a number of other elements arranged around it. The central element provides the core information, the most important part. It unifies the peripheral items in some way, and the peripheral items are dependent on it for their meaning. Most often the relationship between the central element, or 'nucleus', and the peripheral elements, or 'satellites', is one of attribution or identification. The peripheral elements represent the attributes or characteristics of the

# 3

# Loading Paper and Originals

### Loading Paper into the Paper Support

1  Fan the paper.

2  Center the paper on the paper support.

3  Adjust the paper guides so they rest against the edges of the paper.

*Figure 2.12* 'Fan the paper' (from Dell Photo All-In-One Printer 926 Owner's Manual, 2006)

central element, or define its identity. Yet other relations may also link a nucleus and its satellites – what matters more than anything is that the domain or semantic field that is structured by the star principle is consistently about one entity to which all the rest of the information relates.

So while, prototypically, satellites are related to the nucleus by attributive or identifying relations, which are different modes of processes of 'being' and 'having' (see Halliday 1994), they can also be related in other ways, such as different kinds of actions, or activities. An example of the latter occurs, for example, in biographies, in which the central character is the nucleus and his/her identity and attributes, together with the activities s/he is involved in, form the bulk of the information. When a domain is expressed by a text, the main entity, or the nucleus of the star pattern, tends to occur in the beginning, thematic position of the majority of clauses and sentences (Halliday 1994). The entity is the overall focus of the text, which has been referred to as the text's thematic development (e.g. Fries 1981; Martin 1993b).

The star pattern is visualized in Figure 2.13.

Star relations can obtain between a nucleus and only two satellites, or even one. The pattern in which the satellites are arranged is of course what gives this non-linear model its name, but the semantic relations form its most important defining feature. The prototypical attributive or identifying relations are always star relations regardless of how many of them modify, or depend on, the nucleus.

When devising the star pattern, we drew on Halliday (1979) and Kress and van Leeuwen (2007) for inspiration. Halliday (1979) considers the process (realized by the verb) to be the nucleus of the English clause, or simple sentence, with the other constituents – the Actor (most often mapped onto the Subject), the Goal (Object), and the various Circumstantials (Adjuncts) forming the satellites. Kress and van Leeuwen (2007) discuss the star pattern as an important type of visual layout, structuring both images and image–text combinations. They observe that it seems to be more prevalent in East-Asian cultures, whereas Given–New and Ideal–Real structures are more

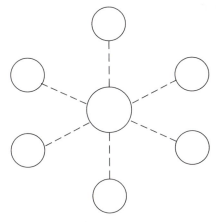

*Figure 2.13* Star

common in Western layouts. Western religious paintings are, however, sometimes also structured by the star principle, as an alternative to the Ideal–Real polarization. In that case, the most saintly character is placed in the central position and those that form the entourage are on the margins. Other kinds of images also exploit the star pattern when needing to show the centrality of one element with respect to others. Figure 2.14 shows two examples of the star organization in images.

(a)

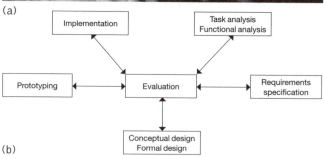

(b)

*Figure 2.14*
(a) *Our Lady of the Immaculate Conception* (Murillo, c. 1678);
(b) Diagram from *Designing the Human–Computer Interface* (Schneiderman 1998)

The role of the star pattern in conveying the meaning of the Madonna's exaltation in Murillo's mediaeval painting is obvious, and further contributed to by the direction of the gaze of the cherubs towards her. The star diagram, on the other hand, expresses the meaning of centrality of evaluation, or user testing, to all the stages in the process of human–computer interface design.

The star organization of information is used at times to structure websites' home pages or CD-ROMs' splash pages, in order to express the centrality of the concept that unifies all the components of the content, or to directly guide the user to the central component. Two examples of the star as the main interface design principle are shown in Figure 2.15.

The European Union's home page has the main concept, that of 'Europa', or the European Union, in the centre, while the countries that made up the European Union

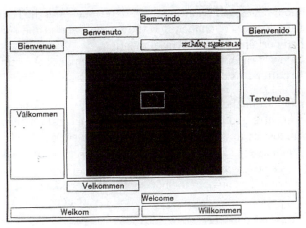

(a)

(b)

*Figure 2.15*
(a) European Union home page;
(b) *Encarta* (Microsoft, 1994) splash page

at the time (November 2001) are represented by the various translations of 'welcome', arranged around the centre. The central position on the *Encarta*'s splash page is occupied by 'Encarta Highlights', which shows the electronic encyclopaedia's designers' (and probably also consumers') idea of what the central element of its content is.

The star format can be combined with the Given–New and the Ideal–Real organization, as Kress and van Leeuwen (2007) have shown. While having the star model as its main form of organization, the *Encarta* splash page in Figure 2.15b is also structured by Given and New: the common ways of navigating content in electronic encyclopaedias (alphabetical index and category browser) are positioned in the left margin, whereas the less usual and more innovative 'gallery wizard' and 'find wizard' are positioned on the right. The European Union's home page could perhaps also be interpreted as having an Ideal–Real organization, alongside the more dominant Centre–Periphery one. Without necessarily wanting to read too much into the form of the layout, the presence of the Romance languages in the top half and of the Anglo-Saxon ones in the bottom half perhaps deserves a brief mention.

The 'Cross' text excerpt below is an example of a domain whose semantic structure is primarily formed by the star pattern, as demonstrated by the analysis in Figure 2.16:

> *Cross* A universal symbol from the remote times; it is the cosmic symbol par excellence. It is a world centre and therefore a point of communication between heaven and earth and a cosmic axis, thus sharing the symbolism of the cosmic tree, mountain, pillar, ladder, etc. The cross represents the Tree of Life and the Tree of Nourishment; it is also a symbol of universal, archetypal man, capable of infinite and harmonious expansion on both the horizontal and vertical planes . . .
>
> (Cooper 1993: 45)

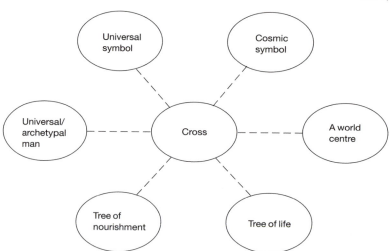

*Figure 2.16* Non-linear analysis of 'Cross' text

A more complex star organization structures the semantics of the following biography, as shown in Figure 2.17.

(About the Author)
Jakob Nielsen, PhD, is a User Advocate specializing in web usability and a principal of Nielsen Norman Group (www.nngroup.com), which he co-founded with Dr D. A. Norman, former vice president of Apple Research. Until 1998, Dr Nielsen was a Sun Microsystems Distinguished Engineer and led that company's web usability efforts starting with the original design of SunWeb in early 1994. His previous affiliations include the IBM User Interface Institute, Bell Communications Research, and the Technical University of Denmark. Nielsen is the author and editor of 8 other books and more than 75 research papers on usability engineering, user interface design, and hypertext. He is also a frequent keynote presenter at industry conferences . . .

(Nielsen 2000)

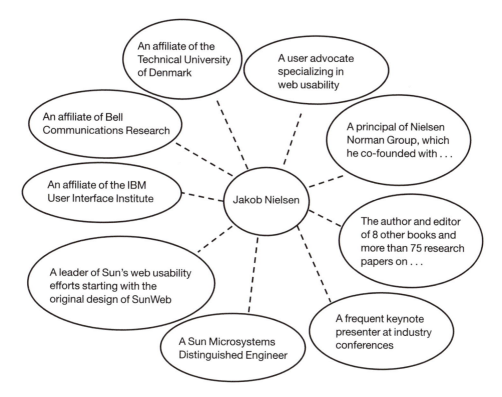

*Figure 2.17* Non-linear analysis of 'Jakob Nielsen bio' text

## The tree (taxonomy)

Trees are non-linear structures that classify items of information into hierarchies. The semantic relationship between the different levels is one of inclusion. There are two basic kinds of inclusion, and therefore two main types of trees. One kind of inclusion is classification, resulting in 'kind of' trees, or classification trees, in which the information in each node is a subtype of the information in the node above. The other kind of inclusion is componential, resulting in 'part of' trees, or componential trees, in which the information in each node is part of the information in the higher node. Some trees consist of nodes linked by both 'kind of' and 'part of' relations.

Trees can be visualized as in Figure 2.18.

Trees have been one of the main tools of organizing knowledge in artificial intelligence (AI). 'Kind of' links have been referred to in AI as 'is a', and 'part of' links as 'part–whole' relations (see, e.g., Lehman 1992). But classification as a principle of knowledge organization has been around for a very long time (see, e.g., Comenius 1658), having found its most prominent expression in the West in the all-encompassing tree of Roget's Thesaurus (first published in 1852), in which much of AI found inspiration.

In this book we draw mainly on systemic analysis of scientific discourse for our conceptualization of trees, and for their realizations in, or extraction from, texts (see, e.g., Wignell *et al.* 1989; Martin 1993a). Further development of this work is found in Kress and van Leeuwen (2007), who consider trees to be types of images. In their system for analysing images, they consider the 'kind of' tree a classificational process, and the 'part of' tree an analytical process.

Trees lend themselves especially well to demonstrating differences between the different forms of organizing knowledge that underlie different views of the world. Commonsense and scientific conceptions of the same or similar domain, for instance, are structurally organized in different ways. Figure 2.19 shows a commonsense classification of diseases (after Martin 1993a).

Medical experts organize this domain quite differently. They do use a classification tree but it relates the various kinds of disease to each other very differently, as shown in Figure 2.20.

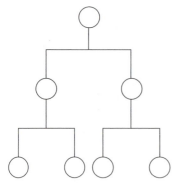

*Figure 2.18* Tree

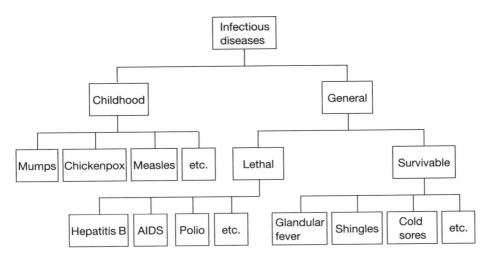

*Figure 2.19* Commonsense classification of diseases (after Martin 1993a)

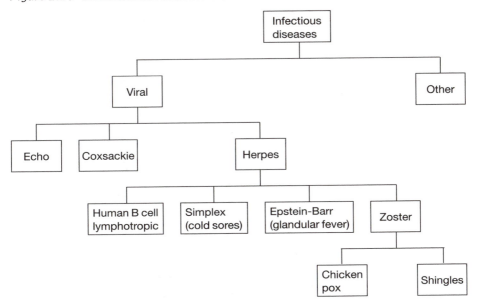

*Figure 2.20* Expert classification of diseases (after Martin 1993a)

Why such a different organization of knowledge in what is essentially the same domain? As Martin (1993a) explains, the classification criteria are different in each case. While the commonsense classification is based on the symptoms and effects of diseases, the expert classification is based on their causes.

Wignell *et al.* (1989) discuss various composition trees, one of which is reproduced in Figure 2.21. As Wignell *et al.* write, this conception of the organization of the body

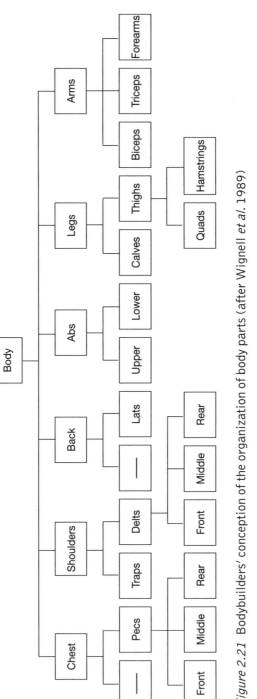

*Figure 2.21* Bodybuilders' conception of the organization of body parts (after Wignell *et al.* 1989)

parts is never explicitly expressed. But it is a knowledge that is implicitly drawn on by any serious bodybuilder and it differs significantly from the way the same domain is organized in the field of anatomy.

As we said in the Introduction, tables of content in books have been used as a metaphor for structuring many websites, with hierarchical structures modelled on the table of contents' chapters, sections, subsections, etc. But usually they are trees only in the sense of the physical inclusion of sections in chapters, and chapters in the book as a whole. When analysed for their semantic structure, they tend to be a combination of several non-linear models. In the Lonely Planet guidebook to the American Southwest (Rachowiecki 1999), the table of contents and the title form one semantic unit, as shown in Figure 2.22.

This can be represented as a set of nodes related by a combination of tree and star relations as shown in Figure 2.23.

*Facts about the Southwest, Facts for the visitor, Introduction* (to the Southwest), *Outdoor activities* and *Getting around* are all about the Southwest, and can all be considered attributes of the Southwest. *Planning, Tourist offices,* etc. are kinds of fact for the visitor, and *History, Geography,* etc. are kinds of facts about the Southwest. *Arizona, Utah* and *New Mexico* are part of the Southwest, and so are the nodes in the composition tree that has the Southwest as its root node. But at the same time, each of them is the nucleus of which *Facts about Arizona, Facts about Utah* and *Facts about New Mexico* are satellites – the relationship between the nodes is that of a star, because the facts are Attributes and the states are the 'Carriers' of these Attributes. The facts about *Phoenix and around* and about the *Grand Canyon & Lake Powell* are more specific facts about Arizona, so these nodes and the *Facts about Arizona* node

# Southwest
### Arizona, New Mexico, Utah

INTRODUCTION
FACTS ABOUT THE SOUTHWEST
History
Geography
. . .

FACTS FOR THE VISITOR
Planning
Tourist Offices
. . .

OUTDOOR ACTIVITIES
. . .
. . .
GETTING AROUND
. . .
FACTS ABOUT UTAH

SALT LAKE CITY
. . .
WASATCH MOUNTAINS REGION
. . .
. . .

FACTS ABOUT ARIZONA

PHOENIX AND AROUND
. . .
GRAND CANYON & LAKE POWELL
. . .
. . .
FACTS ABOUT NEW MEXICO

ALBUQUERQUE AREA
. . .
SANTA FE & TAOS
. . .

*Figure 2.22* Title and table of contents of a Lonely Planet guidebook to the American Southwest (Rachowiecki 1999)

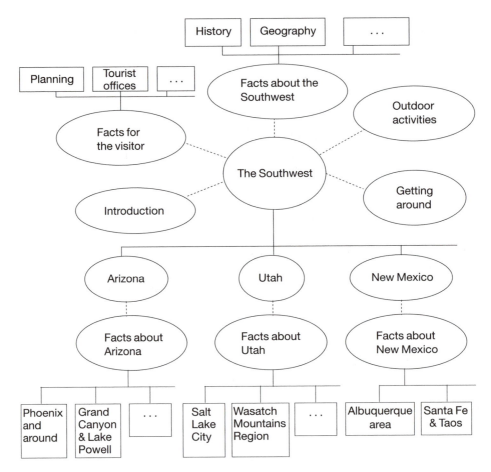

*Figure 2.23* Non-linear analysis of the Lonely Planet guidebook

are in a classification tree relationship, and the same is true of the other facts and *Facts about Utah* and *Facts about New Mexico*.

The 'acid' text excerpt below is quite rich in classifying relations, as can be seen from the tree in Figure 2.24:

> An *acid* is a molecule that releases protons (hydrogen ions) in solution. Conversely, a *base* is a molecule that can accept a proton. Acids and bases can be further divided into strengths. A *strong acid* is an acid that releases all of its hydrogen ions in solution. Hydrochloric acid (HCl) is an excellent example of a strong acid. *Weak acids* are those which do not completely ionize, or lose their hydrogen ions, in solution. The concentration of free hydrogen ions (protons) is referred to as the acidity of the solution.
>
> (www.biology-online.org/9/1_chemical_composition.htm)

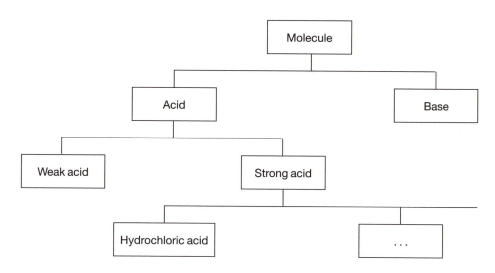

*Figure 2.24* Non-linear analysis of 'acid' text

The 'Arri ST' text below is structured around a componential tree, as represented in Figure 2.25.

> The first 16 mm camera made by this firm was the ST model. The shape of its body is compact and designed for handholding. It houses the intermittent drive mechanism, the reflex viewfinder, and space for the film, while the lens turret is mounted on the front.
>
> INTERMITTENT DRIVE. This mechanism comprises a single-claw shuttle pulling down on one side of the film, and a register pin to steady the film during exposure ( . . . )
>
> REFLEX VIEWFINDER. This type of viewfinder ( . . . ) produces a very bright image, even when the diaphragm is stopped down for shooting. The optical tube gives a 10 x magnification. The eyepiece is adjustable and closed automatically when not in use.
>
> LENS TURRET. The turret takes three lenses with mountings of special design . . .
>
> (Raimondo Souto 1967: 102–3)

## The table (matrix)

Tables are used for comparing different items of information. The entities or processes to be compared are listed vertically. The attributes in terms of which they are compared are listed horizontally. Each entity or process is then described by a

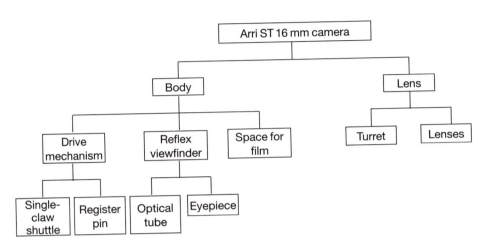

*Figure 2.25* Non-linear analysis of 'Arri ST' text

row of attributes which distinguish it from the other entities or processes. The semantic relationship between the entities/processes and their attributes is thus similar to that between the nucleus and the satellites, and the description of an entity or process is similar to a star. The difference between the two models as a whole is that tables allow a *comparison* of what otherwise might be considered nuclei, in terms of what otherwise might be considered satellites.

The entities or processes to be compared in a table must of course be comparable. This means that they must be of the same kind and of the same level of generality. One cannot meaningfully compare an elephant (a kind of animal) and an orange (a kind of fruit), or browsers and word-processing programs, because it would be difficult to find attributes that would apply to both. But one can compare an elephant and a rhinoceros, or an orange and an apple. The former are both animals, they are both mammals, they are large, etc. The latter are both kinds of fruit, both grow on trees, are edible, and so on. Different kinds of browser can also meaningfully be compared, for example in terms of the features they support, and so can different sorts of word-processing programs (recent comparisons in the press of free web-based packages, such as Writely with MS Word, are a case in point).

As for keeping the same level of generality, it is difficult to compare elephants and animals, since animals are a much broader category and have many attributes that do not apply to elephants. But animals and plants are comparable, and so are elephants and rhinos. What this means is that the entities or processes that are compared in a table should belong to a tree, or taxonomy, and should be at the same tree layer. The table thus appears to be a non-linear model that combines aspects of both a star and a tree, yet it is different from both in its emphasis on comparison.

The familiar shape of the table is visualized in Figure 2.26.

Tables are useful for summarizing often vast and rather complex domains, the semantics of which is predominantly structured around comparison. One such domain is the comparison of the main characters in classical Westerns as written about by Wright (1975). The tabular summary, a conceptual map of the character types in a particular kind of Western, is shown in Figure 2.27. Similar tables for other kinds of Westerns would have different values in the cells of the table.

If the semantics of a particular text or domain is predominantly structured around describing a number of different items by various characteristics, or attributes, a table is a good choice for translating it into a non-linear format. An example is the 'prototyping' text excerpt below, analysed in Figure 2.28.

*Figure 2.26* Table

| | Strong/weak | Good/bad | Wild/civilized |
|---|---|---|---|
| Heroes | Strong | Good | Wild |
| Settlers | Weak | Good | Civilized |
| Bandits | Strong | Bad | Civilized |

*Figure 2.27* Analysis of character types in the Western (after Wright 1975)

| | Purpose | Shelf time | Changes to features |
|---|---|---|---|
| Requirements animation | Possible requirements | | No changes |
| Rapid prototyping | Possible requirements, adequate design | Thrown away | No changes |
| Incremental prototyping | Large systems instalment in phases | | Changes |
| Evolutionary prototyping | Systems construction, evaluation and evolution | Kept | Changes |

*Figure 2.28* Non-linear analysis of 'prototyping' text

Various kinds of prototype have been developed to elicit different kinds of information. One form of prototyping is sometimes called *requirements animation*. Possible requirements (usually functional) are demonstrated in a prototype, which can then be assessed by users. *Rapid prototyping* is also used to collect information on requirements and on the adequacy of possible designs. In rapid prototyping, the prototype is thrown away, in the sense that it is not developed into the final product, although it is an important resource during the project's development. In contrast, *incremental prototyping* allows large systems to be installed in phases to avoid delays between specification and delivery. The customer and supplier agree on core features and the implementation is phased to enable an installation of a skeleton system to occur as soon as possible. This allows requirements to be checked in the field so that changes to core features are possible. Extra, less important, features are then added later. *Evolutionary prototyping* is the most extensive form of prototyping; it is a compromise between production and prototyping. The initial prototype is constructed, evaluated and evolved continually until it forms the final system.

(Schneiderman 1998)

There are two empty cells in the table, which, however, could easily be filled by doing some additional research. Translating linear texts into non-linear diagrams often brings such gaps to light. While writers of linear texts can easily fuzz over them, without their readers noticing, in non-linear forms of representation they are less easily concealed.

We will now briefly comment on the differences between our tables and databases, as databases are also frequently referred to as 'tables'. But databases are tables in a somewhat different sense from the non-linear models we are discussing here. They do have the table structure with independent and dependent variables, but rather than being used to compare entities, they are used for information storage. Any one of our non-linear models could be stored in such a database, the table of course among them, and used in, for example, a multi- or mono-modal (hyper) text generation system, such as described in O'Donnell (2000). But databases are devices for electronically storing information, whereas our tables are devices for modelling a particular non-linear semantic structure, on a par with the tree, the star, the network, and so on.

## The network (web)

Networks are good for showing connections between items of information that are not hierarchical (so they are unlike trees) and that are distributed rather than centralized (so they are unlike stars). They have been designed to include as much information as possible and so the relationship between the nodes in one and the same network can be of many kinds, e.g. 'a is like b', 'a combines with b', 'a co-occurs with b', 'a does something to b', etc. Although network relations are non-hierarchical, some nodes are more important than others, simply by having more links passing

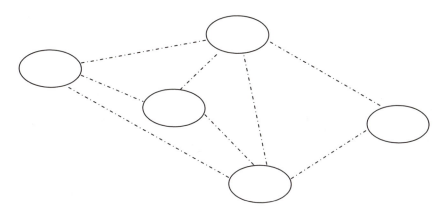

*Figure 2.29* Network

through them. Since network relations are so varied, we will label each of them in our analyses. A simple visualization of a network is shown in Figure 2.29.

The tree, the star and the other simple non-linear model relations can be mixed with network relations and thus form part of larger networks, with none of them being predominant. Networks like these have been used in AI to model knowledge bases. Their flexibility in modelling different kinds of relations as links between entities, or nodes, has made them useful both for clarifying such relations in the minds of designers and for traversing them with computers in natural language generation and other applications. The following network, shown in Figure 2.30, is part of a knowledge base designed to generate texts about museum jewellery pieces (after O'Donnell 2000).

J-999 and J-998 are the jewellery items this network is about, link labels are in italics, and nodes are labelled in plain type. The jewellery pieces and the designer (King) are the most important items in the network, with 4, 5 and 6 links passing through them respectively. The network includes two hierarchical classification relations.

The semantics of some complex domains may be best expressed by one of the basic non-linear models we have discussed so far, with others playing a subordinate role. Such models can be joined together as in Figure 2.23 or they can be linked by network relations in an overall, complex non-linear model (see Chapter 3). Networks are thus the most flexible of the non-linear models, and are useful for mapping out the semantics of the most complex domains.

Network diagrams have often been used to represent physical networks, such as the internet infrastructure network (see, e.g., The Atlas of Cyberspaces, www. cybergeography.org/atlas/atlas.html). Figure 2.31 shows the London Underground network.

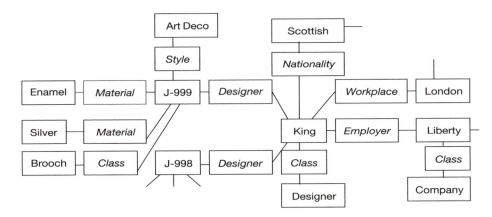

*Figure 2.30* Jewellery network (after O'Donnell 2000)

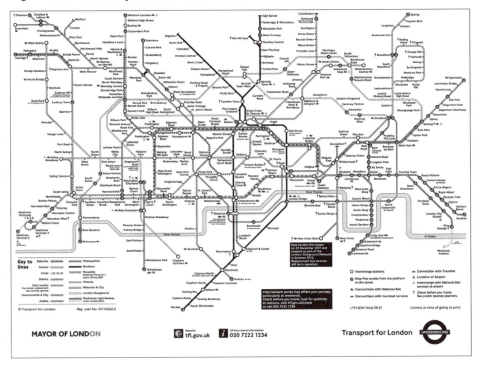

*Figure 2.31* London Underground network

Obviously stations like Kings Cross-St Pancras and Baker Street are more important in the underground's transport structure because they have more lines going through them than stations such as Putney Bridge.

The 'new inscription' text excerpt below is an example of a text best translated by a network structure:

One of Britain's leading lettercutters, Richard Kindersley, cut this R in brick as a trial for a large architectural inscription. Lettering artists such as Kindersley have pioneered a whole range of new inscriptional styles and techniques. These are of special interest to architects and the designers of retail outlets. Slate, marble, limestone, granite, wood, and even man-made materials are suitable for chisel-cut letters. These need not remain in architectural settings, but can be included as photographic images in designs for print.

(Neuenschwander 1993: 131)

As analysed in Figure 2.32, the text centres on 'new inscriptional styles and techniques', and in that sense it is organized according to the star pattern. Chisel-cut letters are a kind of new inscriptional styles and techniques, and are related by network relations to their settings and materials. Different designers (lettering artists, architects, and designers of retail outlets) connect to these techniques in different ways: the lettering artists produce them, and the architects and retail outlet designers 'are interested' in them. Finally, other network relations link the letter R to Kindersley on the one hand and to brick on the other.

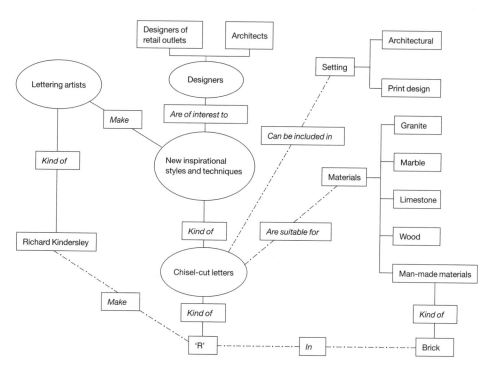

*Figure 2.32* Non-linear analysis of 'new inscription' text

# 3  Complex non-linear models

Complex non-linear models combine several simple non-linear models. Knowledge domains of any complexity are bound to be structured by complex models. In such cases, one of the simple models tends to be the main one and the others are of secondary importance, linked or joined to it, and at times to each other as well. When mapping out a domain or translating a text into a non-linear format, the model that accounts for the most information in the domain or text should be chosen as the main model. As we said in the Introduction, the choice of non-linear models is usually moti-vated by the designer's goal or strategy, or by that of the organization for which s/he works. Translating linear texts into non-linear formats, however, means that the goals of these linear texts were already decided upon in advance by their writers. As we will show later in this chapter, all texts have strategies encoded in their lexical and grammatical patterns, and designers/translators should base their interpretations on these patterns. In most cases they will not be able to question the writer of the text, who in any case may not be fully conscious of his or her goals. They will therefore have to rely on the lexical and grammatical patterns that encode the intention of the text (Eco 1992). Although their goals or strategies are limited by the text's inten-tions in this way, designers/translators can influence the inclusion or exclusion of some of the subordinate models in the resulting complex non-linear model. In other words, they can select the level of detail of the analysis.

In this chapter we will analyse the semantic structure of three texts, each one of them lending itself to being translated primarily by a specific non-linear model.

## The tree as the main non-linear model

To demonstrate the translation of a linear text into a complex non-linear model whose main component is a tree, we have chosen a passage from a book about the history of Western music. In our method, this kind of translation is the first step towards designing a new media product, in this case a new media product aimed at making users understand and appreciate different kinds of early polyphonic music. Samples of the music would of course eventually have to be added, but the basic underlying structure would be conceptual – a mind map of mediaeval music.

> As regards the two main ways of singing in parts – namely, the exact repetition of a melody at different pitches to suit different voices (parallel organum) and the simultaneous ornamentation of a melody (free organum) – it was, as we should expect, the latter which caught on, for the desire to ornament or vary given

material is and always has been a much more powerful one than that which merely aims at duplication.

The most arresting thing about free organum is the use of contrary motion, and although neither the ninth-century authors of *Musica enchiriadis* and *Scholia enchiriadis* nor Guido of Arezzo in the eleventh century especially stress this, Guido at any rate seems to prefer free to parallel organum, and some of the examples he gives not only employ contrary motion, but crossing of parts as well; furthermore, the collection of over 150 two-part organa from Winchester which are contemporary with Guido contain a number of passages in contrary motion, particularly at cadences. Thus one of the two essential characteristics of polyphony – melodic independence – had entered music, and round about 1100 the great theorist who is usually called John Cotton and described as an Englishman, but who was almost certainly a monk at the Flemish monastery of Afflighem, near Liège, specifically recommended contrary motion and the crossing of parts. In so doing he advocated using all the concords, not just parallel fourths or fifths, as the theorists before him had done, but a mixture of unisons, fourths, fifths, and octaves, all the other intervals being regarded as discordant as before, and therefore only to be used as approaches to concords.

The second of the two essential characteristics of polyphony – rhythmic independence – can also be found in some of Guido's examples, where several notes of the chant melody or vox principalis are set against one note of the vox organalis, and although later practice reversed this procedure by setting several notes of the organalis to one of the principalis, the seed had been sown, and again we find John of Afflighem strongly recommending what had previously only been allowed. But rhythmic independence inevitably demanded some kind of measuring system if the parts were to be sung or played as the composer wished. So long as the parts moved at the same time there was no difficulty in keeping together, but when, as happened at the beginning of the twelfth century, the chant melody was performed in long-drawn-out notes above which was added a florid organalis part, the problem of ensemble became serious. Admittedly the music was written in score with one part above the other, and the vertical alignment of the notes would give an approximate indication as to how many organalis notes were to be sung to one of the principalis, but the exact point at which the principalis changed from one 'held' note to the next (hence the name, 'tenor', from the Latin *tenere* = 'to hold') can only have been decided by the choirmaster. Assuming of course, there was an 'exact point', because while accurate ensemble matters to us it may not have mattered to the early composers of organa provided that certain 'rules' were observed, such as beginning and ending a phrase on a concord.

(Harman and Mellers 1980: 44–6)

We represent the semantic structure of this text by the non-linear diagram shown in Figure 3.1.

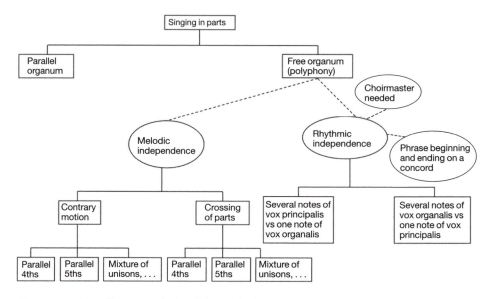

*Figure 3.1* Non-linear analysis of the 'polyphonic music' text

There are two main kinds of organization in this text. One is chronological and charts the main stages in the evolution of polyphonic music. The other is a more static, conceptual structure of polyphonic music that can be extracted without regard for the chronology of the stages of introduction of the various concepts. Since we are dealing with static conceptual structures, or non-linear models, in this book, we disregard the chronological structure. This is not to say that it is not important but it is not the focus of our analysis. It could in any case be brought in at a later stage, if we decided to combine the conceptual structure with a more dynamic perspective on the text.

The conceptual structure of the 'polyphonic music' text is organized around a classification of *singing in parts*. Two main kinds are first identified, *parallel organum* and *free organum*. Parallel organum is abandoned more or less immediately, as a less interesting way of making music, and the rest of the text is devoted to free organum, or polyphony. In the second paragraph, free organum is described as having the essential attribute or characteristic of *melodic independence*. This we therefore represent as a satellite linked by a star relation to the nucleus of *free organum*. Melodic independence is then said to be of two kinds: *contrary motion* and the *crossing of parts*, which are therefore related to melodic independence as subordinates to a superordinate in a classification tree. At the same time, contrary motion and the crossing of parts are themselves of different kinds – those that use *parallel 4ths, parallel 5ths*, and a *mixture of unisons, 4ths, 5ths and octaves*, which results in another two classification trees.

The last paragraph introduces the second essential attribute of polyphony, which is *rhythmic independence*, and it specifies two kinds of it: *several notes of vox principalis versus one note of vox organalis*, and *several notes of vox organalis versus one note of vox principalis*. The rest of the paragraph is rather complex, but in the simplest possible analysis, its representation can be reduced to two attributes – the *need for a choirmaster* and the *phrase beginning and ending on a concord* – linked by star relations to rhythmic independence.

The diagram in Figure 3.1 represents only the bare bones of the conceptual organization of the text. All we seek to do here is present or identify the different ways of singing in parts and the various characteristics of polyphony, so as to bring together the key information in a clear and coherent semantic structure. Including the satellites that specify the *need for a choirmaster* and for the *phrase beginning and ending*

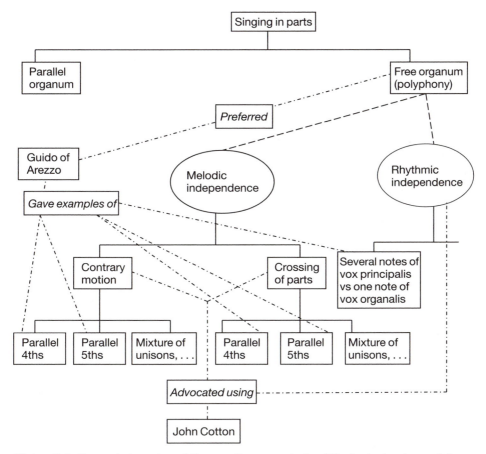

*Figure 3.2* Expanded version of the non-linear analysis of the 'polyphonic music' text

*on a concord* already goes beyond this most basic goal, because these satellites are about the problems that arose because of rhythmic independence. However, much more information could easily be added. This would be motivated by the designer's strategy, and, ultimately, by the characteristics of the target audience. The designer may want to provide more contextual information, for instance about the theorists (Guido of Arezzo and John Cotton), and these could be linked by network relations to the polyphonic features with which they are associated. Figure 3.2 shows what the relevant parts of the overall diagram would then look like.

As we have already mentioned, the extraction of a complex model from linear text is of course not just intuitive but based on the way the non-linear models have been encoded in the grammar and lexis of the text. To begin with, the first paragraph of a text usually outlines what the rest of the text will be about. The first sentence of each paragraph then tends to outline what the rest of the paragraph will be about, and the first clause in a sentence usually outlines what the rest of the sentence will be about (see Martin 1993b). When we see an expression like 'the two main ways of singing in parts' in the first paragraph of the text, we know that what follows will be concerned with classification. The rest of the paragraph, however, makes clear that only one of the ways of singing in parts will be dealt with in any detail, which means that a star pattern is likely. This is confirmed by the presence of *free organum*, or polyphony, in the first (very long) sentence of the second paragraph, and also in the first sentence of the third paragraph. The two main organizing principles of the semantic organization of this text are thus the classification tree and the star.

The expressions 'one of the two essential characteristics of polyphony – melodic independence' in the second paragraph and 'the second of the two essential character-istics of polyphony – rhythmic independence' in the third paragraph make it clear that the star is indeed the best model here and that these two expressions are satellites. A clue to the further classification of melodic independence into contrary motion and the crossing of parts is found in the second paragraph, especially in 'some of the examples [*of free organum*] he [*Guido*] gives not only employ contrary motion, but crossing of parts as well . . . Thus one of the two essential characteristics of polyphony – melodic independence – had entered music'. Similarly, 'In so doing [*recommending contrary motion and the crossing of parts*] he [*Guido*] advocated using all the concords, not just parallel fourths or fifths . . . but a mixture of unisons, fourths, fifths, and octaves . . . ' gives a clue to the further subclassification of both contrary motion and the crossing of parts. The classification of rhythmic indepen-dence into two kinds is encoded at the beginning of the third paragraph, namely in 'where several notes of the chant melody or vox principalis are set against one note of the vox organalis, and although later practice reversed this procedure by setting several notes of the organalis to one of the principalis . . . '.

We will now present and critique some of our students' translations of the 'poly-phonic music' text. Figure 3.3 shows one of these.

The main problem with this diagram was the modelling of *free organum* and *polyphony* as separate nodes. According to the text, the two are one and the same

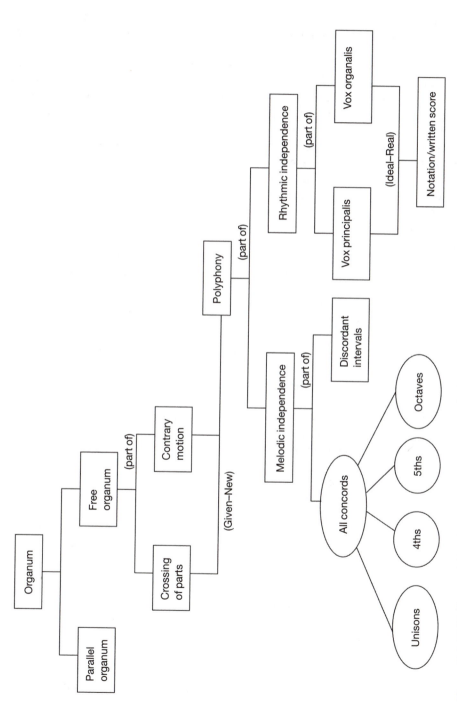

*Figure 3.3* Will, Sue and Katy's non-linear analysis of the 'polyphonic music' text

thing and there should therefore be only one node for both in the diagram. *Crossing of parts* and *contrary motion* are not really part of *free organum* either. Componential relations are deceptively easy to identify and use, and it is usually best to keep them for modelling relations between physical entities since otherwise they result in a lack of clarity in the non-linear model. Although it could be argued that *crossing of parts* and *contrary motion* are 'part of' *free organum* as they somehow belong to it or tend to appear in the same context, this is a rather loose way of defining the relationship. According to the text, free organum/polyphony has two main characteristics, melodic independence and rhythmic independence, and contrary motion and crossing of parts are two kinds of melodic independence. Our students used componential relations here to suggest that melodic independence and rhythmic independence are somehow 'part of' polyphony but that, again, is a little too vague. A star relationship is best in this context since it makes clear that melodic and rhythmic independence are attributes of polyphony.

The diagram also used a componential relationship to link *vox principalis* and *vox organalis* to *rhythmic independence*. This was a misunderstanding of the concepts themselves and of their relations. First of all, the subordinates are not *vox principalis* and *vox organalis* but *several notes of vox principalis versus one note of vox organalis* and *several notes of vox organalis versus one note of vox principalis*. Secondly, these two concepts are kinds of, rather than parts of, rhythmic independence, so the tree should be a classification tree rather than a componential tree. The last componential tree relationship in the diagram links *all concords* and *discordant intervals* to *melodic independence*, and there are several problems with this too. First of all, there is no need for an *all concords* superordinate to the *parallel 4ths and 5ths* and a *mixture of unisons*, and the text says nothing about *discordant intervals* having anything to do with *melodic independence*. As well, the classification tree relationship outlined in the text between a *mixture of unisons* and the *parallel 4ths and 5ths* on the one hand, and the *crossing of parts* and *contrary motion* on the other, is missed. Finally, the Given–New relationship between *crossing of parts* and *contrary motion* on the one hand and *polyphony* on the other does not make much sense. It was obviously meant to account for the two former concepts appearing on the left of the page and the latter concept on the right, but that is a purely coincidental result of the way the diagram is drawn. Given–New is a semantic relation, which means that it would make sense in this context only if somehow crossing of parts and contrary motion preceded polyphony in the history of music, which they do not. The same applies to the Ideal–Real relationship in the diagram between *notation/written score* on the one hand and *vox principalis* and *vox organalis* on the other. This again seems to be motivated by the former concept appearing underneath the two latter concepts, which has nothing to do with their semantic relationship.

After a tutorial with one of the authors, the students redrew the diagram, as shown in Figure 3.4.

This version fitted the semantics of the text much better, although there was still room for improvement. The form of the diagram, for example, did not make any

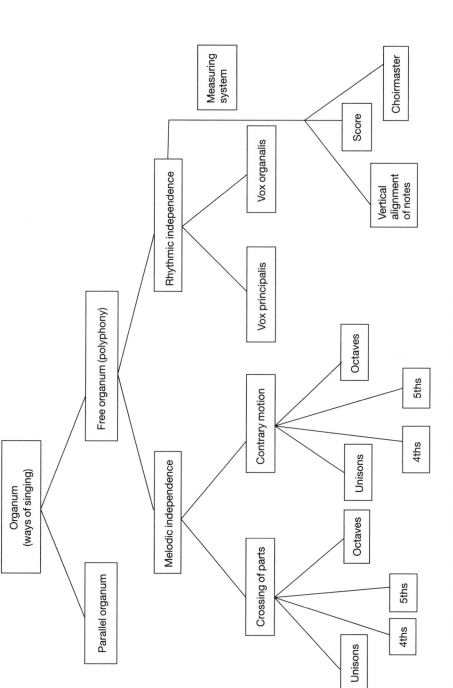

*Figure 3.4* Second version of Will, Sue and Katy's analysis of the 'polyphonic music' text

distinction between tree relations and star relations, both of which are represented by the same kind of slanted lines. And the concepts that are subordinate to *rhythmic independence* were still not correctly represented. Finally, the network relationship between *rhythmic independence* and the three kinds of *measuring system* was not correctly represented and not formally distinguished from the other relations. An amended, final diagram alleviated most of these problems, as shown in Figure 3.5.

Another group of students produced a more complex translation of the 'polyphonic music' text, including some network and some table relations (see Figure 3.6).

Although much thought went into this translation, the result was perhaps too complicated, mostly because of the students' excessive use of network relations. Like componential tree relations, network relations should be used sparingly and only when the other kinds of relations have been exhausted. They are a little too easy to use, and since they are so varied and so little constrained, they often result in a less rigorous mapping of the semantics of a text than could be achieved by drawing on the more clearly defined classification tree, star and other relations. There is, for example, no need for a 'result in' network relation between *contrary motion* and *crossing of parts* on the one hand and *melodic independence* on the other. As well, it is not clear from the diagram whether *free organum* and *polyphony* are considered to be the same concept or not, and that ambiguity should be resolved. This should lead to the realization that *contrary motion* and *crossing of parts* are really kinds of *melodic independence*. Another network relation – 'occurs through' – would then fall by the wayside, too. Finally, a more rigorous analysis would identify *vox principalis* and *vox organalis* as having to do with *rhythmic independence* along the lines already described in relation to the previous group's diagram. The network relation labelled as 'occur together' would then also be eliminated.

There are two useful network relations in the diagram, however: *John Cotton – recommends – free organum* and *rhythmic independence – requires – measuring system*. Both are motivated by realizations in the text which would be difficult to translate into other non-linear models.

There were a few other problems with this diagram. The title itself needed to be changed since the text is about 'singing in parts' of which polyphony, or free organum, is only one kind, the other being parallel organum, or homophony. *Score, improvisation rules* and *choirmaster* are all kinds of *measuring systems* and so this relationship is one of classification and should be expressed by a tree. The relationships between the concepts in the table with John Cotton are better expressed as a Given–New structure (kinds of melodic independence used before John Cotton and after John Cotton). The relationship between *Guido of Arezzo* and *organum* was not specified. Lastly, according to the text, *florid organum* is not really at the level of free and parallel organa but only a melodic line sung above the chant melody in twelfth-century polyphony. Figure 3.7 shows how the students revised the model after a tutorial with one of the authors.

The network relations labelled *added* that were used to link *score* with *choirmaster* and *improvisation rules* make sense, since, according to the text, score by itself was

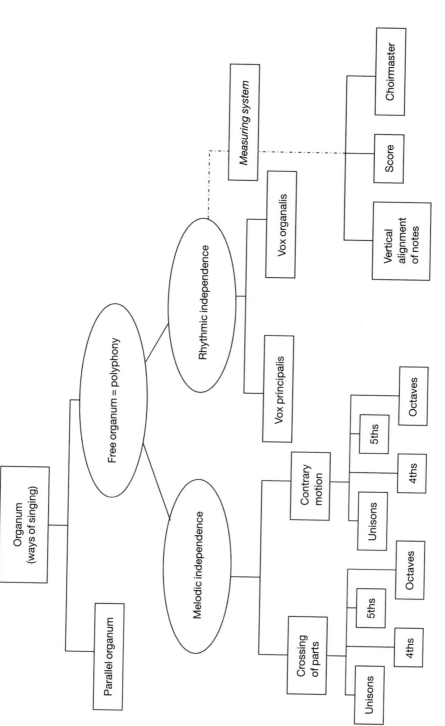

*Figure 3.5* Final version of Will, Sue and Katy's analysis of the 'polyphonic music' text

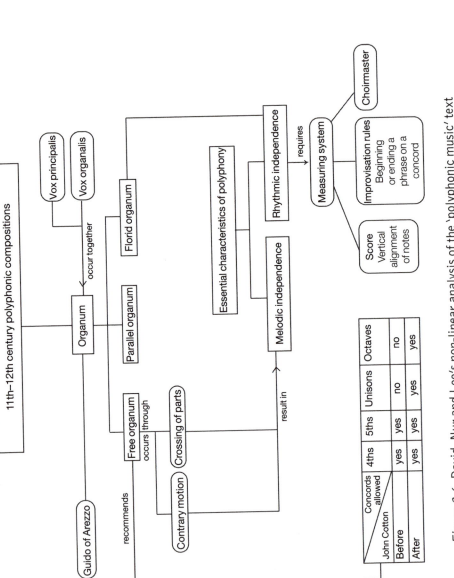

*Figure 3.6* David, Nur and Lee's non-linear analysis of the 'polyphonic music' text

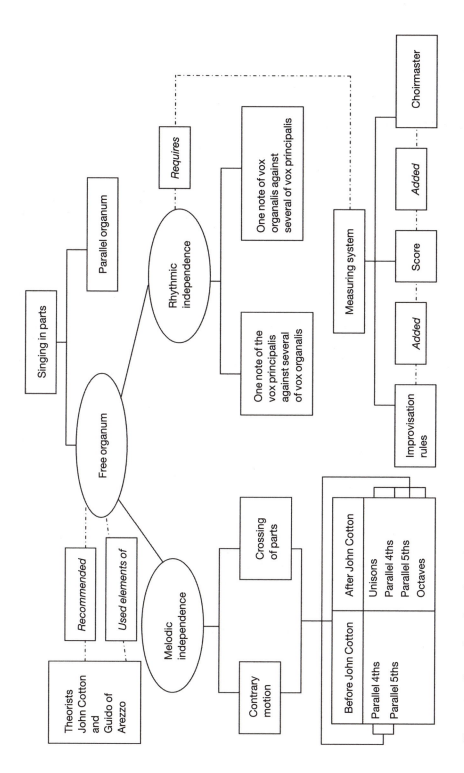

*Figure 3.7* Second version of David, Nur and Lee's analysis of the 'polyphonic music' text

not sufficient for the performers to keep time, which had to be determined by the choirmaster or was kept track of with the help of improvisation rules.

## The table as the main non-linear model

The linear text we chose to translate into a complex non-linear model centred on a table is a passage from a book about Art Deco jewellery:

> The men and women of the Twenties were obsessed with the passing of time. 'Live fast', the leitmotiv of the *Années Folles*, gave the watch a role of primary importance. Jewelers instantly understood the capital they could make out of this useful object. The mechanisms were made by the specialized watchmaking industries of the Franche-Comte in France, or in Switzerland, and the jewelry designers then took charge of transforming this object into a piece of jewelry or a luxury object. The fate of the watch was thus closely linked with the art of *bijouterie-joaillerie*.
>
> Mechanical advances and the miracles accomplished by the watchmaking craftsmen furnished the jewelers with infinitely small and curiously *calibré* movements which they then took pleasure in decorating. While in the eighteenth century, the watch, with its chatelaine and hanging ornaments, had offered large surfaces for decoration with enamel, diamonds and gemstones, the inverse occurred with the production of miniaturized mechanisms. Ladies' watch-bracelets, invented towards the end of the eighteenth century, were launched anew by jewelers at the beginning of this century. They became more popular, along with bracelets, when feminine fashion no longer required long sleeves and when participation in sport required a more functional jewelry. From the first watch-bracelets on their moiré or figured patent leather straps, to those sparkling with stones; from the most modest to the most lavish, the designer-creators devised an infinite number of variations whose vast range is an indication of the support of their clientele. If the watch-bracelet was to be acceptable with evening dress it had to be gorgeous enough to take place next to other bracelets. The watch case, often very narrow, was set with precious stones, diamonds or pearls, and the dial was reduced to microscopic dimensions. The Maisons created diamond bracelets at the centre of which a tiny watch was concealed: the movement was in platinum and the crystal which covered the dial was emerald-cut to look like a large gem. Other models took the form of supple straps of gold or jewels whose central part opened like the lid of a box to reveal the dial.
>
> Competing, between 1925 and 1930, with the watch-bracelet, the pendant- or chatelaine-watch was all the rage at a time when evening dresses were short on one side and long on the other. They were one of the most popular creations of Van Cleef et Arpels and Laclocke. The forms of these watches were fanciful in the extreme and the dial was often invisible, sometimes hidden in a pearl tassel, as in the case of one of Cartier's models.

Another variation was the watch-brooch. Only the owner of this piece of jewelry knew that it was a brooch that told the time, for the dial remained hidden. The motifs of these brooches were often figurative, but always typical of Art Deco, as for example, in a design by Marchak which took the form of a vase of flowers in diamonds and coloured stones whose front opened to reveal the watch. Another model by Bourdier represented a diamond mill whose façade tipped up when the catch was released to reveal the minuscule dial. The watch, symbol of the active life, invaded other objects: it nestled in cigarette boxes, in lipstick cases, in powder compacts, in dressing cases or vanity cases. And inventive richness went into the design not only of ladies' watches, but also of men's, the watch being one of the few pieces of jewelry, together with tie-pins and cuff links, to which men were entitled. The wrist watch arrived and, practical as it was, began to take preference over the pocket watch. The list of watch creations by Cartier and Boucheron over the years reveals their imaginativeness and their astonishing capacity for renewing forms and combining new materials. When little shuttered watches appeared, disguised in a gold watch case in the form of a lighter, the fob watch was, literally, liberated from its chain. The movement of these watches was revealed when the two shutters were opened and the watch thus became a miniature bedside or desk clock. The watches were decorated with lacquer or with mother-of-pearl encrusted with coral. Cartier created a similar model, the slide-action pocket watch, where the rectangular enameled watch case, which covered the dial, opened as pressure was applied at the sides. If the growing demand for watches brought with it mass-production by the watchmaking industries – Lip, Longines and Auricoste – the jewelers' watches were, nevertheless, distinguished by the refinement and luxury of their materials and by the fact that certain models were unique, designed and conceived for a single client, or produced in limited editions.

(Raulet 1985: 78–81)

Our own solution for mapping out the semantic structure of this text is shown in Figure 3.8.

The main portion of the text compares different types of watches designed in 1920s Paris in terms of their various characteristics, or attributes. The non-linear model that captures the most information in this text and that is the most faithful to its semantic structure is thus the table. The first paragraph sets up the context for the comparison, but is not part of the comparison itself and therefore does not appear in the table. The influence of the socio-cultural context on watchmaking is dealt with in a Given–New structure linked to the table, which will be discussed further below.

In the second paragraph the *pendant* or *chatelaine* watches popular in the eighteenth century are compared with the *ladies' watch bracelets* invented at the end of the same century and relaunched at the beginning of the twentieth century. The comparison is in terms of the materials used (*enamel, diamonds* and *gemstones* for the pendant watches, and *patent leather, precious stones, diamonds, gold, pearls,*

|  | Materials | Decoration | Forms | Dials | Manufacturers | Sex |
|---|---|---|---|---|---|---|
| Watch bracelets | Patent leather, precious stones, gold, pearls, platinum, crystals | Moiré, figured | Bracelet | Microscopic | Maisons | F |
| Pendant/ chatelaine watch | Enamel, diamonds, gemstones | | Pendant/ chatelaine, fanciful in the extreme | Often invisible | Van Cleef et Arpels, Lacloche, Cartier | F |
| Watch brooch | Diamonds, coloured stones | Figurative Art Deco | Vase, mill | Hidden, small | Marchak, Bourdier | F |
| Invasive watches | | | Nestled in cigarette boxes, lipstick cases, powder compacts, dressing cases, vanity cases | | | F, M |
| Wrist-watch | New materials | Imaginative | New forms | | Cartier, Boucheron | M |
| Pocket watch | Gold, enamel | Lacquer, mother of pearl, coral | Lighter with shutters, rectangular slide-action | Hidden | Cartier, Lip, Longines, Auricoste | M |

| | |
|---|---|
| Living fast, active life | Watch becoming of primary importance |
| Mechanical advances and miracles accomplished by watchmaking craftsmen | Infinitely small and curiously *calibré* movements |
| Feminine fashion no longer requiring long sleeves | Watch bracelets becoming popular |
| Participation in sports | More functional watch bracelets: figured patent leather |
| Evening dress | Gorgeous watch bracelets: precious stones, diamonds, pearls, gold, platinum, crystals, jewels |

*Figure 3.8* Non-linear analysis of the 'Art Deco watches' text

*platinum* and *crystals* for the watch bracelets), in terms of the form of the whole watch (*pendant* or *chatelaine* as opposed to *bracelet*), in terms of decoration (*moiré* or *figured* for the bracelet watch, with that of the pendant watches not mentioned) and in terms of the dials (*microscopic* for the bracelet watch and *often invisible* for the pendant watch). There is also information about the maker of the bracelet watches (*Maisons*).

The third paragraph describes the new version of the chatelaine watches in some detail. It specifies their manufacturers (*Van Cleef et Arpels, Lacloche* and *Cartier*), their forms (*fanciful in the extreme*), and their dials (*often invisible*). In the fourth paragraph, the *watch brooch* and its attributes are first discussed. The *dial*, which was *hidden*, the form (*figurative Art Deco*, e.g. a *vase of flowers, mill*), the materials (*diamonds, coloured stones*), and the manufacturers (*Marchak, Bourdier*). Then *invasive* watches are mentioned, which were placed, or cased, in *cigarette boxes, lipstick cases, powder compacts*, and *dressing* or *vanity cases*. This is followed by a brief mention of men's wristwatches – of the new materials they were made of, their new forms, and their imaginative decorations. Two manufacturers are also mentioned (*Cartier* and *Boucheron*). The fact that men's wristwatches are being discussed (rather than women's) has to be inferred from the mention of *men* in the preceding sentence, and from the wristwatches taking over from *pocket watches* that were only worn by men. After this, *men's pocket watches* are discussed in some detail – the materials they were made of (*gold, enamel*), their form (*a lighter with shutters, rectangular slide-action*), decoration (*lacquer, mother of pearl encrusted with coral*) and dial (*hidden*). Finally, watch manufacturers are mentioned (*Cartier, Lip, Longines, Auricoste*).

As for the lexical and grammatical realizations of the table in the text, most of it is through lexis, as traced in the preceding several paragraphs. One clue to the table's being the overall model for the text is that the second paragraph, which is about watch bracelets, is followed by a paragraph that discusses pendant/chatelaine watches and begins with 'Competing . . . with the watch-bracelet, the pendant- or chatelaine-watch'. This wording could theoretically set up a classification tree as well, with *watch bracelets* and *chatelaine/pendant watches* as two nodes subordinate to a *watch* node, but the fact that there is so much descriptive information about watch bracelets suggests a comparison in terms of attributes, and therefore a table. This is further confirmed by 'Another variation [of the watch] was the watch-brooch' in the next paragraph, followed by a description of its attributes, and by a gradual introduction and description of other types of watches.

There is of course much information in the text that is not included in the table. But a selection had to be made. This is one of the principles of analysing a complex text like this. The best thing to do is to read the text through and consider how it is structured as a whole. What is its most dominant overarching structure? It is important not to get mired in detail. Including all the information in a non-linear model would be a next to impossible task and lead to an overwhelmingly complex network which would miss the most important generalization, namely that the text is fundamentally a comparison of different kinds of watches.

It is important to be selective when identifying the characteristics in terms of which the various watches are compared. We selected only the attributes that apply to all the watches in the table. For example, the attributes of the watch case were mentioned in the second paragraph, in relation to the watch bracelets, and then again in the fourth paragraph, in relation to pocket watches, but never in relation to the other four watch types included in the table. So we left out the watch case attribute. We could of course have done more research on these attributes to allow us to fill the cells that apply to them as well. Similarly, the *manufacturers* attribute could have been divided into luxury watch manufacturers and mass-production manufacturers, but although this distinction is made in the final sentence of the text, the text as a whole is only about luxury watches and does not discuss examples of mass-produced ones. In all this we took the minimalist approach and tried to stay as close to the text as possible. The resulting table therefore has only a minimum number of holes – each column has at least 4 out of the total 6 cells filled, and each row at least 5 out of 6. The only exception is *invasive watches* about which only very little information is provided in the text.

As mentioned above, there is a good deal of information in the text that we have not included in the final table. It could, however, be expressed by other non-linear models, and these could then be linked to the table by network relations. What to include or not depends on the designer's strategy and ultimately on the target audience. A designer wanting to create a new media product that would simply compare types of watches in terms of their attributes could include just the table itself. This might be appropriate for a target audience of watchmakers. In the second translation, the table could still be translated differently, again depending on the target audience. A group of watchmaking experts specializing in Art Deco watches, for example, might be quite happy with a format that actually looks like a table. They would already know what the particular watches look like and perhaps appreciate a no-frills design that allows them to compare the characteristics of different watches at a glance. Less specialized watchmakers might prefer a more covert translation in which each row of the table is translated by images as well as more detailed descriptive information.

If the designer/translator wanted to include the social and historical context of the rise in popularity of the watches, the Given–New model could be added, alongside the table. A new media product based on such a complex non-linear model would be more educational, and thus more appropriate for a target audience of watchmaking students who still need to familiarize themselves with the impact of context on the design and manufacture of watches. The selection of the second translation of this complex non-linear model would again be motivated by a choice between more finely differentiated target audiences. This time, the age dimension would most likely be relevant. Older students might prefer an introduction which would just provide the facts about the context. It could be formed by a sequence of images juxtaposed with text excerpts about the social and historical characteristics of the context and their influence on watch design. Younger students would probably prefer a more entertaining and metaphorical second translation in the form of some narrative scenario.

Although the relationship between the Given and New items in the diagram appears to be a cause–effect relation, it can also be seen as a temporal relation, since the changes in social context preceded the effects they had on the development of watch-making. Network links connect items within the New with related cells in the table. The exact parts of the New entries that are related to the table cells are underlined. *Infinitely small and curiously calibré movements* relate to the whole *dials* column, because all the watch dials that are discussed in the article were small, which was enabled by the tiny movements. *Watch bracelets* relate to the whole *watch bracelet* row in the table. *Figured patent leather* relates to *figured* in the decoration cell, and to *patent leather* in the *materials* cell, since it only applies to watch bracelets of that subtype. *Precious stones, diamonds, pearls, gold, platinum, crystals and jewels* only relate to *precious stones, diamonds, pearls, gold, platinum, crystals and jewels* in the *materials* cell because they are related to that kind of watch bracelet.

We will now critically discuss some of our students' translations of the 'Art Deco watches' text, starting with a group that translated the text as a star with trees attached to the satellites (see Figure 3.9).

This was a good translation, strongly motivated by textual realizations and logically very consistent. It is certainly true that most sentences in the text begin either with watches or things to do with watches, such as their manufacturers, the materials they are made of, their types and mechanisms. The various aspects of watches are then further developed along different lines which could be represented as different classes of materials, manufacturers, etc. And these could be seen as being further subclassified into various types. The problem with this kind of translation, however, is that the most important meaning, which applies to the text most comprehensively, the meaning of *comparison*, gets completely sidelined. The text becomes a simple description of various aspects of watch design, and that is not actually its main point.

Another group used a tree to model the same text, as shown in Figure 3.10.

The most important contrast in this classification tree was that between women's and men's watches. Everything else depended on this. There is of course the even more basic distinction between mass-produced watches and jewellers' watches but only jewellers' watches are discussed in any detail in the text. We do not think that the textual realizations support the notion that the contrast between women's and men's watches was the main intention of the text. Men's watches are only mentioned for the first time in the last quarter of the text, and if the meaning of this contrast was so important, it would have been set up earlier, and the amount of text dedicated to each of the two kinds of watches would have been more or less equal. Our comment on the preceding (star and trees) translation of the same text applies here as well: the meaning of comparison is lost when the text is translated as a tree. Finally, a tree translation is less economical than a table translation, since many of the lower-level nodes in all the trees are identical, which results in a great deal of repetition (e.g. *dial, materials, covered, uncovered, Maisons, Cartier*, etc.). Such repetition is a good indication that a table is really what is called for, since that is the model which naturally captures the description of various entities by the same variables.

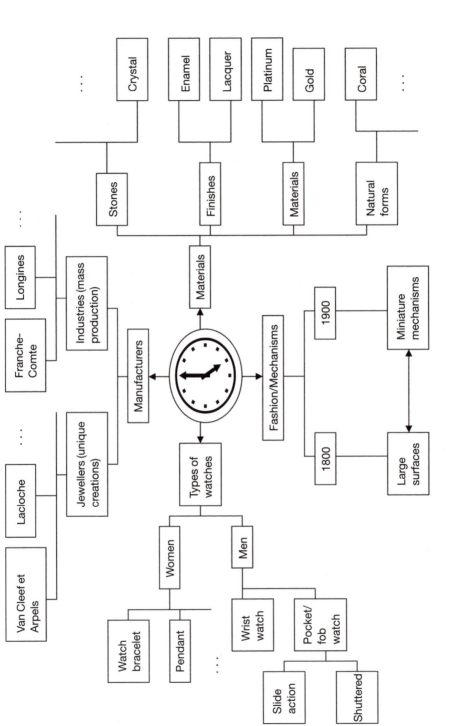

*Figure 3.9* Maryam, Jane and Rirette's non-linear analysis of the 'Art Deco watches' text

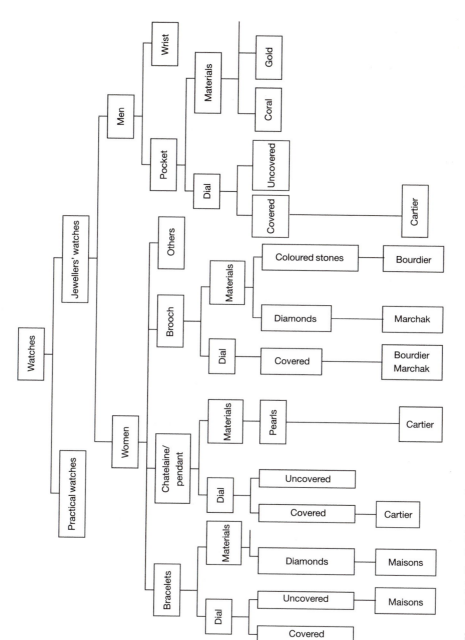

*Figure 3.10* Rudi, Rigel and John's non-linear analysis of the 'Art Deco watches' text

One of the more interesting translations of the 'Art Deco watches' text was the one shown in Figure 3.11.

This complex non-linear model combines the classification tree and the table. The students clearly understood that the independent variables in a well-formed table should all belong to the same layer of a classification tree. However, there was no need to make the tree explicit. Art Deco watches could simply have been used as a heading for the independent variables column and the understanding that in a well-formed table the independent variables all have to be of the same kind and level of generality could have remained implicit. The third layer of the tree in Figure 3.11 consisted of a classification of the different watch types by manufacturer, which brought up another problem, namely an increased number of empty cells (e.g. the decoration of Van Cleef et Arpels and for Lacloche pendant watches, the dial of

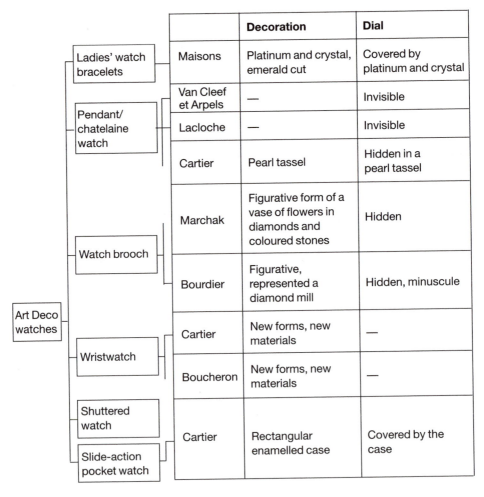

| | | Decoration | Dial |
|---|---|---|---|
| Ladies' watch bracelets | Maisons | Platinum and crystal, emerald cut | Covered by platinum and crystal |
| Pendant/ chatelaine watch | Van Cleef et Arpels | — | Invisible |
| | Lacloche | — | Invisible |
| | Cartier | Pearl tassel | Hidden in a pearl tassel |
| Watch brooch | Marchak | Figurative form of a vase of flowers in diamonds and coloured stones | Hidden |
| | Bourdier | Figurative, represented a diamond mill | Hidden, minuscule |
| Wristwatch | Cartier | New forms, new materials | — |
| | Boucheron | New forms, new materials | — |
| Shuttered watch / Slide-action pocket watch | Cartier | Rectangular enamelled case | Covered by the case |

Art Deco watches

*Figure 3.11* Christina, Rachel and Mohamed's analysis of the 'Art Deco watches' text

Cartier and Boucheron wristwatches), as the information in the text is incomplete in this respect. The issue of excessive repetition also needs to be mentioned here, e.g. the invisible dial of both Van Cleef et Arpels and Lacloche pendant watches or the hidden dial of both Marchak and Bourdier watch brooches.

Finally, some of the attributes did not represent the descriptions of the watches in the text very well, and some others were missing. *Materials,* for example, should have been separated from *decoration* because the two are independently variable – figurative decoration, for instance, can be produced with either diamonds or coloured stones. And some of the entries listed under *decoration* were really materials that are used for other purposes than decoration, e.g. platinum is used to make the watch movement. Finally, the *sex* attribute could have been added, since, although not the most important one, it does play a role in the comparison of watches in the text – men's watches are compared with women's watches in terms of the inventive richness of design.

Yet another group included both a table in which the watches were compared and a Given–New structure which mapped out the influence of the social context of the 1920s on watchmaking. The two non-linear models are presented in Figure 3.12.

The table is quite similar to the one in Figure 3.8, so we will not discuss it in detail. Some aspects of the Given–New model however deserve a mention. First of all, based on the text, *accessory object* in the Given should have been changed to something like *watch as everyday object* since the New is *jewellery object*. This would have made it clearer that this instance of polarization is about a change in status and quality of watches during the 1920s. Secondly, the *jewellers – mass production watch industry* pair should have been left out since it is of a different kind from the rest. The other pairs of concepts are all related by a relationship that could be worded as 'leading to' – e.g. *live fast (active life) – popularity of watch, change in fashion (long sleeves) – different models of watches (day/evening), sports – functional watches,* etc. The *jewellers – mass production watch industry* pair is related by a simple contrast. The context in which this contrast is made is the growing demand for watches and the concurrent demand on the part of rich consumers to distinguish themselves from the crowd. The two concepts could have easily been included in the table instead, by subdividing the *manufacturers* attribute into two columns.

The students' diagram does not show how the Given–New model and the table should be combined to form a complex non-linear model. This is also a shortcoming, and one which could have easily been remedied. *Different models of watches (day/ evening)* in the New could have been linked to the *chatelaine or pendant watch* in the first column of the table, since according to the text the chatelaine or pendant watch was worn with evening dresses. *Functional watches* should have been linked with the *watch bracelet* because, as the text says, watch bracelets became popular when feminine fashion no longer required long sleeves and when participation in sport required more functional types of jewellery. *Miniaturized mechanism* could have been linked to *watch bracelets* since the text strongly implies that they were used in their production, but most of the other types of watches are also good candidates. And, following

| Given | New |
|---|---|
| • Live fast (active life) | • Popularity of watch |
| • Change of fashion (long sleeves) | • Different models of watches (day/evening) |
| • Sports | • Functional watches |
| • Accessory object | • Jewellery object |
| • Mechanical advances | • Miniaturized mechanism |
| • Jewellers | • Mass-production watch industry |

| | Materials | Decoration | Form | Dial | Manufacturer | Watchcase | Sex |
|---|---|---|---|---|---|---|---|
| **Chatelaine or pendant** | Pearl tassel | Enamel, diamond, gemstones | | Invisible, hidden | Van Cleef et Arpels, Lacloche, Cartier | | Women |
| **Bracelet** | Moiré leather straps, stone, platinum, crystal | Gold, precious stones, diamonds, pearls | Small, emerald cut, like a large gem | Microscopic dimensions | Maisons | Very narrow | Women |
| **Brooch** | Diamonds, coloured stone | Art Deco, figurative | Tiny | Hidden or minuscule | Marchak, Bourdier | | Women |
| **Slide-action pocket watch** | Diamonds, gold | | Rectangular | | Cartier | Enamel, covered the dial | Men |
| **Wristwatch** | Leather, metal | Art Deco | | | Lip, Longines, Auricoste | | Men/women |

Figure 3.12 Brogan, Philip and Janet's analysis of the 'Art Deco watches' text

the text, *watch as jewellery object* could have been linked to the *bracelet* and the *brooch*.

As we will see in Chapter 4, the network relations between the Given–New model and the table, although not represented in the diagram, were translated very creatively in the actual new media product based on this model. The Given–New structure was translated as a Flash introduction with slow-moving images of the 1920s social context, e.g. of a woman in an evening dress in front of a typically Parisian background or of women of the era playing tennis, alternating with sentences representing the Given–New relations, e.g. *New trends in fashion lead to changes in watch design* or *Increasing participation in sports makes the wristwatch popular*. The first column of the table that contains the watch types was translated as the first-layer navigation menu, made up of images of the watch types drawn in red ink. And the connection between the introduction and the navigation menu was made by the watches worn by the people in the slow-moving photos turning into the red-ink drawings and rising to the top of the page where they formed a horizontal navigation bar.

## The star as the main non-linear model

The text we chose to demonstrate translation into a complex non-linear model with a star at the first level of structure is a passage from a sociology book about violence and the rise of the nation state:

> The pike was in turn gradually overtaken by weaponry that harnessed the explosive force of gunpowder, surely one of the most momentous technological changes in human history. The gun had some very profound consequences for the shaping of modern civilization because, in the shape of early artillery, it helped sharply reduce the significance of the castle and the city as containers of military power. A gun is an 'industrial' device in the sense which that term has when applied to the Industrial Revolution. That is to say, it is a mechanical artifact whose impetus depends upon the application of inanimate sources of material energy.
>
> The Spanish armies were the first to use guns in large measure among the infantry. Something like a sixth of their foot soldiers in the Italian Wars carried guns; the majority, however, remained pikemen. A variety of explosive weapons were tried but the two main ones early on were the ten-pound, four-foot arquebus and the fifteen-pound, six-foot musket. By the middle of the sixteenth century the two-man musket, fired from a forked rest, had become the leading weapon; it fired a two-ounce ball that could penetrate all existing forms of armour, and had a range of some three hundred yards. A great deal of other equipment had to be carried to make the guns work, which they might in any case refuse to do in bad weather. However, their use promoted tight discipline, because something like a hundred separate movements had to be carried out in order to achieve any sort of rapid firing. The concentrated fire-power of ranks of men demanded even more stringent and routinized co-ordination.

Field artillery quickly became a significant factor in laying siege, and its very immobility helped shift the locales of battles away from concentration on castles and cities – the vanquishing of an army on open terrain would allow the artillery pieces subsequently to be brought into action against fixed fortifications if needed. New types of fortification that were invented to counter explosives had no particular connection with urban areas. The gun as well as gunpowder may well have originally been a Chinese invention but the European development of them, under the pressure of more or less continuous war, moved far ahead. Gustavus Adolphus (who with Maurice of Nassau must rank as the greatest innovator among military leaders in the absolutist period) was responsible for two major contributions to military technology. He was among the first to carry on sustained winter campaigns, something which was made possible by the alterations he made in the modes of military transportation and supply. But he also helped invent a new cartridge which, together with a lightened musket-barrel, made the field gun considerably more portable. Loading and reloading became significantly quicker, with the result that new battlefield formations could be achieved, heightening the offensive capabilities of the gun-carrying troops in relation to others. The subsequent invention of the flintlock and the bayonet decisively turned warfare in the modern direction. The former greatly augmented the rate of fire, while the second made the gun-carrying soldier simultaneously a pikeman. The days of the massed ranks of pikemen were then over.

(Giddens 1996: 107–8)

Our representation of the semantic structure of this text is shown in Figure 3.13.

Like the 'polyphonic music' text and, to some extent, also the 'Art Deco watches' text, this text intersperses a historical narrative with a more static, conceptual structure. The narrative will be ignored for now, but as in the case of the 'Art Deco watches' text, parts of it could be included in the non-linear diagram, and consequently in the new media product based on it. Reading through the entire text, it becomes clear that its conceptual structure is about one central item of information, namely *guns*. Everything else is directly or indirectly related to it. The most suitable non-linear model to form the centre of the complex model is thus the star. Let us attempt to construct the star model first then. *Guns* (or *the gun*) are what the text is about and they therefore form the nucleus of the star. This nucleus has five main satellites, i.e. chunks of information that relate to guns.

The first satellite is mentioned in the first paragraph, namely the consequences of guns for the shaping of modern civilization. The second satellite is introduced in the second paragraph, namely the types, or varieties, of guns. The third satellite is also set up in the second paragraph, and it has to do with the consequences of guns for the shaping of modern warfare. This satellite is not made explicit in the second nor indeed the following paragraph, but the first such more specific consequence is discussed at the end of the second paragraph, which is the effect of the two-man musket on the promotion of tight discipline and co-ordination. Other such more specific conse-

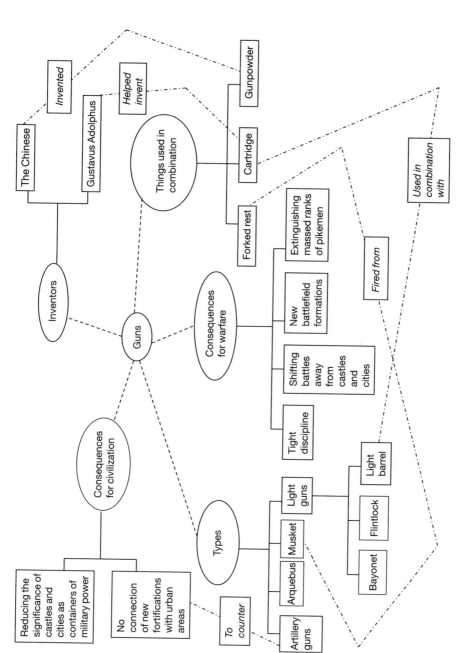

*Figure 3.13* Non-linear analysis of the 'guns' text

quences of guns for the shaping of modern warfare are introduced in the third paragraph: the shifting of battles away from castles and cities, new battlefield formations, and the extinguishing of mass ranks of pikemen. Since all these are kinds of consequences of guns for warfare, they justify the setting up of a superordinate item, the consequences of guns for warfare, which is at the same time a satellite of the guns node.

Another satellite, the things that were used in combination with guns, is introduced in the first paragraph and then developed further in the second and the third. The satellite itself is again not explicitly mentioned but three such more specific things are: gunpowder (paragraphs 1 and 3), the forked rest (paragraph 2) and the cartridge (paragraph 3). They thus form the subordinate nodes of a classification tree whose superordinate node is *things used in combination (with guns)*. Finally, the last satellite of the *guns* nucleus is discussed, namely the inventors. There are two examples of them, the Chinese and Gustavus Adolphus (both in paragraph 3), who thus form the subordinates of the *inventors* node.

While discussing the satellites of *guns*, we could not avoid the trees that further subclassify the *consequences (of guns) for warfare*, *things used in combination (with guns)*, and *inventors* satellites. But the remaining two satellites, *consequences (of guns) for civilization* and *types (of guns)* are similarly subclassified. The first kind of *consequences for civilization* is *reducing the significance of castles and cities as containers of military power* (paragraph 1) and the second *no connection of new fortifications with urban areas* (paragraph 3).

As for the kinds of guns which subclassify the *types* node, these are *artillery guns* (paragraphs 1 and 3), *arquebus* (paragraph 2), *musket* (paragraph 2), and *light guns* (paragraph 3). The two satellites, *consequences for civilization* and *types*, are thus also joined to classification trees. Finally, the important parts of the light guns are discussed in the third paragraph, namely *light barrel*, *flintlock* and *bayonet*. These thus form the subordinate nodes of a composition tree, whose superordinate is *light guns*.

The non-linear diagram discussed so far maps out most of the semantic structure in the 'guns' text. But several network links could be added, specifying several significant connections between the nodes of this complex non-linear model. The first network link makes explicit that the new types of fortifications that had no connection with urban areas were invented in order to counter the effects of the artillery (see paragraph 3). The second network link shows that it was the musket that was fired from a forked rest (paragraph 2). Another two network links make clear that the gunpowder was invented by the Chinese (paragraph 3), and that Gustavus Adolphus helped invent the cartridge (paragraph 3), and the last network link specifies that the cartridge was used in combination with the light barrel.

As in the case of the 'polyphonic music' and 'Art Deco watches' texts, we had to be selective. Had we tried to include all the details, the resulting complex non-linear model would have been cluttered and the overall semantic pattern would have been missed. Being selective of course means that whatever information is included in the final diagram is ultimately a matter of interpretation. However, as we have already said, this does not mean that the selection is arbitrary. It remains firmly grounded in the lexical and grammatical structures of the text. When lexical items like *gun* and *guns*, and the more specific items that are their subordinates (*musket, arquebus, artillery guns*, etc.), are mentioned repeatedly throughout the text alongside other, related, items like *gunpowder, flintlock, bayonet*, etc., this is a good indication that the whole text is about guns and that *guns* is therefore the nucleus of a star pattern which forms the main, overall semantic organization of the text. This is especially so when guns in general, as well as their various subordinates, superordinates and synonyms frequently appear in the thematic (initial) position of the sentences and clauses. Examples include *the gun* (sentence 2), *a gun* (sentence 3), *it [a gun]* (sentence 4), *explosive weapons* (sentence 7), *their [guns'] use* (sentence 10), *fire-power* (sentence 11), *field artillery* (sentence 12), etc.

The interpretation of the structure of this semantic field is thus very much circumscribed by the lexical and grammatical patterns in the text. Different patterns realize different non-linear models. Once a text is written, its non-linear semantics has already been selected. Deciding to write a passage about the classification of light guns, for instance, will necessarily involve developing an extended taxonomy, or tree, throughout a series of paragraphs, rather similar perhaps to the classification of polyphonic music in the 'polyphonic music' text. This tends to be the case, too, with the texts that usually form the basis for designing websites or information systems in the industry – whether they be company briefs or records of designer–client interviews.

Apart from the expressions that realize the main star form of organization in the 'guns' text, there are various others which indicate the presence of other non-linear models. When coming across 'a variety of explosive weapons were tried' (paragraph 2), one can reasonably expect that some kind of a classification of these weapons will be carried out in the passage or passages that follow. Thus a tree is likely to be set up. Another classification is likely to follow a clause like 'the gun had some very profound consequences for the shaping of modern civilization' (paragraph 1). The clause sets up an expectation that the different kinds of consequences are going to be discussed later in the text, especially since it is in the first paragraph.

The whole text, excluding the chronological, narrative aspect, can thus be conceptualized as one large semantic field to do with guns, which includes smaller semantic fields to do with their consequences for civilization and for warfare, their types and inventors and whatever things were needed to make them function.

We will now discuss some of our students' translations of the 'guns' text. One such translation is shown in Figure 3.14.

This was a fairly good translation although some aspects of it needed to be modified. First of all, the non-linear model had the form of a big tree. But looking at the labelled nodes, it is obvious that not all the relations are tree relations. The *properties, types, contributors* and *social effects* nodes are in fact related to the *guns* node by star relations. *Guns* is thus the nucleus of a star and the other nodes are its satellites. The satellite nodes are simultaneously superordinates of other, subordinate nodes. The first-level subordinates of *types* and *social effects* are quite

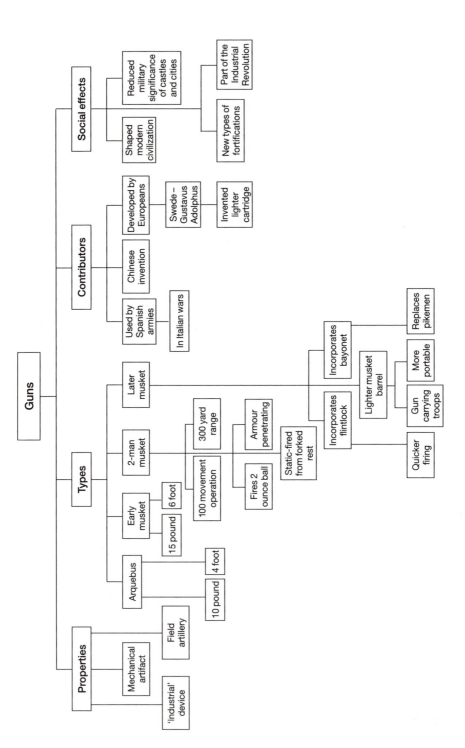

*Figure 3.14* Jennifer, Kylie and Richard's translation of the 'guns' text

straightforwardly related to them by classification tree relations. The subordinates of the *properties* node are, however, not quite right. *Field artillery* should really be a subordinate of *types* of guns. '*Industrial*' *device* and *mechanical artifact* are so closely related that it does not make sense to consider them subordinates of a classification tree. They are found in the following passage (paragraph 1):

> A gun is an 'industrial' device in the sense which that term has when applied to the Industrial Revolution. That is to say, it is a mechanical artifact whose impetus depends upon the application of inanimate sources of material energy.

If anything, *mechanical artifact* is a more general term than '*industrial*' *device* and should therefore be its superordinate.

The *contributors* 'tree' also needed correction. If we keep *contributors* as the super-ordinate and preserve all the content it contains, the first-level subordinates should be *the Chinese* and *the Europeans*. The subordinates of *the Europeans*, in turn, should be *Gustavus Adolphus* and *Spanish armies*. A network relation labelled *invented* should then lead from *Gustavus Adolphus* to *lighter cartridge* and another labelled *in* should lead to *Italian wars*.

In the *types* tree, *10 pound* and *4 foot* are satellites of *arquebus* to which they are related by star relations. The same is true of *15 pound* and *6 foot*, and *early musket*. And it is equally true of all the concepts that appear below *2-man musket* and the *2-man musket* term itself. The *later musket* tree should be remodelled as follows: *flint-lock, bayonet* and *lighter barrel* should be related to *later musket* by componential tree relations. A network link labelled *enabled* should lead from *lighter barrel* to *quicker firing* (another one from *lighter cartridge* in the *contributors* tree also leads to *quicker firing*). A network link labelled *made more portable* should lead from *lighter barrel* (and another one from *lighter cartridge* in the *contributors* tree) to a new node labelled *the field gun*. Finally, another network link labelled *replaced* should lead from *bayonet* to *pikemen*.

After a tutorial with one of the authors, the students created the revised complex non-linear model reproduced in Figure 3.15.

This version of the diagram was much more rigorous than the previous one, although several details still needed altering. First of all, the *social effects* non-linear model is not really a star but a classification tree – *new types of fortification, shaping of modern civilization*, etc. are all kinds of social effects. We also had reservations about the subordinates of the *definitions* tree, and the whole tree could probably be left out without much being lost. Finally we thought that the network link leading from *lighter musket barrel* should be labelled *makes more portable* and lead to a node labelled *the field gun*.

The 'guns' text translation in Figure 3.16 was rather different from what we expected.

Making sense of this diagram was difficult because the students did not indicate the meaning of the lines connecting the nodes, and we therefore could not know what

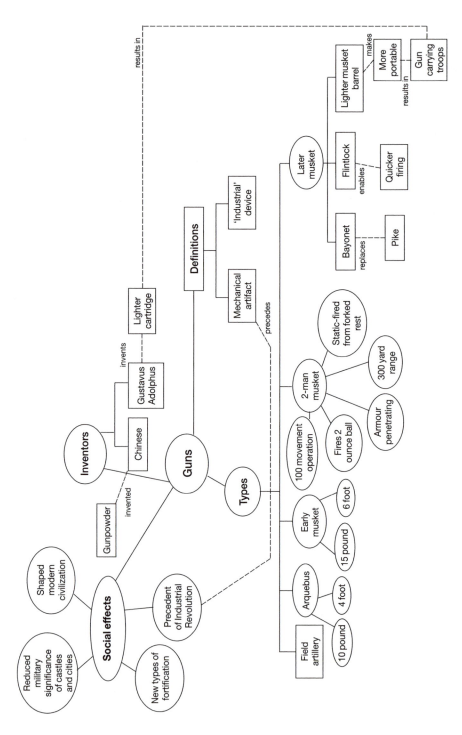

*Figure 3.15* Jennifer, Kylie and Richard's revised analysis of the 'guns' text

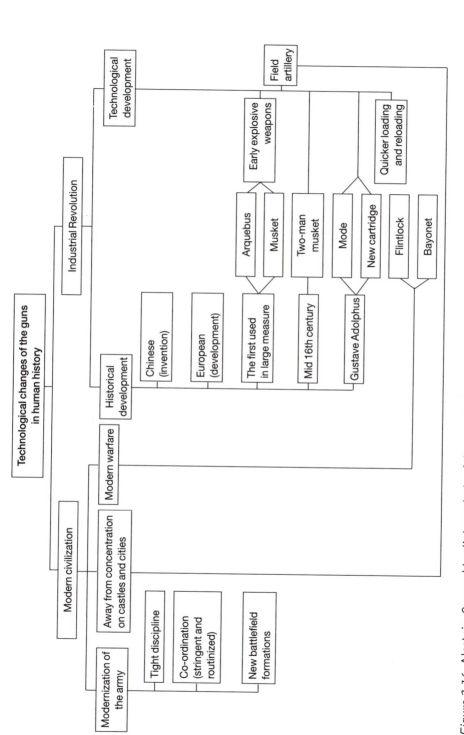

*Figure 3.16* Alastair, Guy and Leslie's analysis of the 'guns' text

non-linear models these lines were meant to represent. Trying to figure out the non-linear semantics of the diagram with the help of the original text, we concluded that the label on the main node (apparently the root node of a tree) was meant to be based on the first sentence of the text, although it appeared to be somewhat misunderstood – according to the text, the process of guns taking over from the pike was one of the most momentous changes in human history. The node could thus perhaps be relabelled as something like *changes engendered by guns in human history*. This main node is related to the first-level nodes, *modern civilization* and *Industrial Revolution*, by what seems to be a classification tree relationship. According to the text, the above-mentioned change (or, more simply, just *guns*) had profound consequences for the shaping of modern civilization. The *modern civilization* node could thus probably be relabelled as *shaping modern civilization*. The *Industrial Revolution* label on the second node is too broad for the semantic field that is intended (based on the diagram's lower-level nodes' labels). According to the text, 'a gun is an "industrial" device in the sense which that term has when applied to the Industrial Revolution', which of course does not mean that the Industrial Revolution was engendered by the invention of the gun or by its taking over from the pike. Yet this is the impression given by the label on the second node.

Proceeding with the second level of the diagram, *modernization of the army*, [*shifting the locales of battles*] *away from concentration on castles and cities* and *modern warfare* could be considered to be subordinates of *shaping of modern civiliza-tion* in a classification tree. It is not clear, on the other hand, how *historical develop-ment* and *technological development* are related to *Industrial Revolution*. Based on the nodes that follow, it would appear that the students assumed that the invention of the gun engendered a small industrial revolution of its own. The nodes seem to attempt to map out what this revolution's main stages were. The two lines leading downwards from *historical development* and *technological development* are therefore temporally rather than conceptually based. This of course is a problem, since the non-linear models we had asked the students to focus on were conceptual rather than temporal (narrative) models.

The nodes that are below the second-level *modernization of the army* node, namely *tight discipline*, *co-ordination (stringent and routinized)* and *new battlefield forma-tions*, could be considered kinds of *modernization of the army* and thus subordinates in a classification tree relationship with that node. The link between [*shifting the locales of battles*] *away from concentration on castles and cities* and *field artillery* is obviously a network link, *field artillery* – *lead to* – [*shifting the locales of battles*] *away from concentration on castles and cities*, and should be so labelled. Finally, *modern warfare* is also linked to *flintlock* and *bayonet* by a network relationship, [*the invention of the*] *flintlock and bayonet* – *resulted in* – *modern warfare*, and should also be labelled accordingly.

After a tutorial with one of the authors, the students created the very different diagram reproduced in Figure 3.17.

The new diagram was much closer to the non-linear semantics of the 'guns' text,

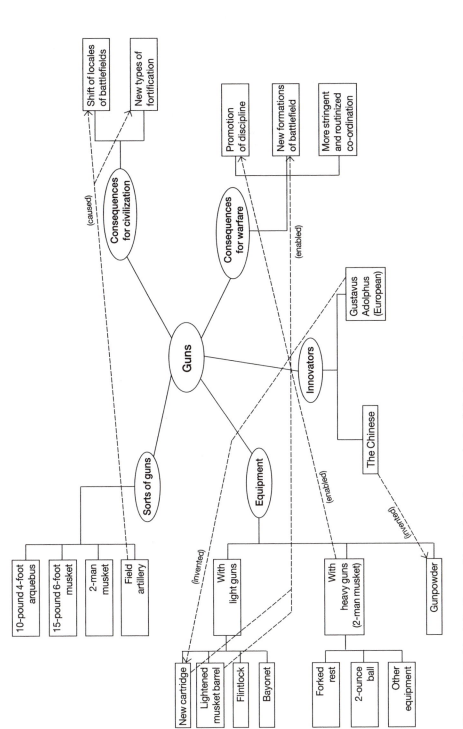

*Figure 3.17* Alastair, Guy and Leslie's revised analysis of the 'guns' text

and was in fact one of the best we received. Two aspects deserve special mention: the considerable number of network relations and the *equipment* tree. The network relations are very useful since they integrate the various simple non-linear models that make up the complex model by showing relationships between their nodes. As we will see in Chapter 4, this group's translation of the network relations into links in the final product was quite interesting and useful. One network relation that could have been improved on is *equipment used with heavy guns – enabled – promotion of discipline*, which, following the 'guns' text, could have been labelled more accurately as *equipment used with heavy guns – promoted – tight discipline*, but that is admittedly a detail. Also, a network link could have been added between *2-man musket* and *forked rest*: *2-man musket – was fired from – forked rest*. As for the *equipment* tree, it makes a nice distinction between equipment used with light guns and equipment used with heavy guns.

# 4 The second translation

Our first translation was a translation from linear texts into the non-linear models that map out, or make explicit, their non-linear underlying semantic structure. The next step in the design process is what we call the 'second translation' – the translation of this non-linear model into an actual new media product such as a website. This translation consists of two stages. The non-linear model is first turned into a non-linear storyboard and then into the new media product itself. But because there is usually little difference between the storyboards and the products, we will, in this chapter, focus only on the new media products themselves.

It is important to note that both translations are grounded in observable features of the texts that are being translated. Just as our first translation was motivated by the lexical and grammatical patterns of the linear text, so our second translation will be motivated by the structure of the non-linear model that is being translated into the new media product. In what follows we present a number of conventions, or rules, that should be followed in order to translate the non-linear models in a way that preserves their meaning. Some of these derive from print and have been used by 'old media' designers for a long time. Others are more recent and specific to the new media.

## Implicit and explicit translations

Second translations can be implicit or explicit. Implicit translations convert all or part of the non-linear model back into linear text. Figure 4.1 shows a non-linear model of the 'guns' text produced by a group of students, and Figure 4.2 shows a screen from the new media product they derived from it.

The *bayonet – replaces – pike* network relation, shown bottom right in Figure 4.1, is translated into the first of the three paragraphs on the left of Figure 4.2: 'Bayonet, which was a knife or dagger shaped weapon that fit on or over the musket muzzle. This essentially replaced the need for Pikemen, infantry who carried pikes (pole weapons with steel tips).' Similarly, the translation of the *flintlock – enables – quicker firing* link, also seen bottom right in Figure 4.1, becomes the second paragraph on the left of Figure 4.2: 'Flintlock Mechanism, which contains a hammer tightly holding a shaped bit of flint. This mechanism resulted in much quicker firing.' Finally, the *Gustavus Adolphus – invents – lighter cartridge – results in – gun carrying troops* and *lighter musket barrel – makes – more portable – later musket* (our addition) *– results in – gun carrying troops* relations, found on the right in Figure 4.1, are translated in the third paragraph of the text in Figure 4.2: 'Lighter musket barrel, which together

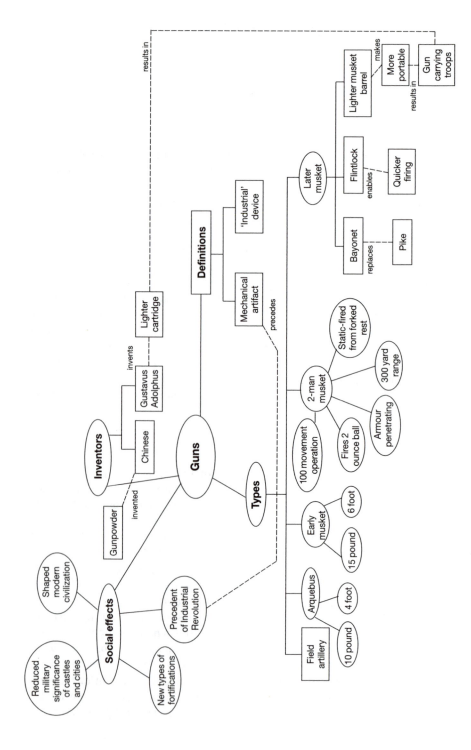

*Figure 4.1* Jennifer, Kylie and Richard's non-linear model of the 'guns' text

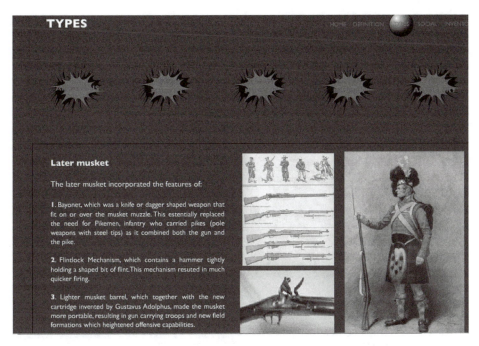

*Figure 4.2* A screen from Jennifer, Kylie and Richard's 'guns' product

with the new cartridge invented by Gustavus Adolphus, made the musket more portable, resulting in gun carrying troops.' In each case the non-linear representations are reconverted into discursive prose.

This implicit method of translating network relations contrasts with explicit translations into navigation links that are usually realized by clickable underlined wordings (clickable images can also be used). We call this method explicit because here the nodes of the non-linear model are translated into actual screens or parts of screens, and the relations between them become navigation links. However, as we have seen, network relations are semantically variable. They can mean 'a is associated with b', 'a does b', and so on (where 'does' can be substituted by any 'doing', or narrative process). The precise nature of these relations cannot be expressed just by moving from one page to another. It therefore has to be expressed in the text or the visuals of the page from which the link proceeds. This is what happens with the two interlinked screens from a student 'guns' website shown in Figures 4.3 and 4.4.

The relation *Gustavus Adolphus – invented – new cartridge* in this group's non-linear model (shown in Figure 3.17 in the previous chapter) is retranslated into language as 'He also invented a new cartridge [which, together with a lightened musket barrel, made the field gun considerably more portable]' in the text below the image of Gustavus Adolphus in Figure 4.3. *New cartridge* in the above sentence is emboldened, creating a link leading to the page shown in Figure 4.4 which features

*Figure 4.3* Screen from 'guns' product by Alastair, Guy and Leslie

an image of the more portable field gun, together with a text that more or less repeats the text on the previous page: 'Gustavus Adolphus invented a new cartridge which, together with a lightened musket barrel, made the field gun considerably more portable, with the result that new battlefield formations could be achieved.' It would have been possible to find a more creative solution than the more or less verbatim repetition of the original text, but the principle would have been the same: network relations realized by verbs are translated within texts, and clickable wordings in these texts translate the nodes on either side of the relations in the non-linear model. In the case of the Gustavus Adolphus page, *new cartridge* is clickable, and in the case of the 'new cartridge & lightened musket barrel' page, *Gustavus Adolphus* is clickable (and leads back to the page shown in Figure 4.3).

The translation of another network relation from the same complex non-linear model, *lightened musket barrel – enabled – new battlefield formations*, can be found on the 'new cartridge & lightened musket barrel' page (Figure 4.4). The translation is '[Gustavus Adolphus invented a new cartridge which,] together with a lightened musket barrel, made the field gun considerably more portable, with the result that *new battlefield formations* could be achieved'. There is a link from the emboldened

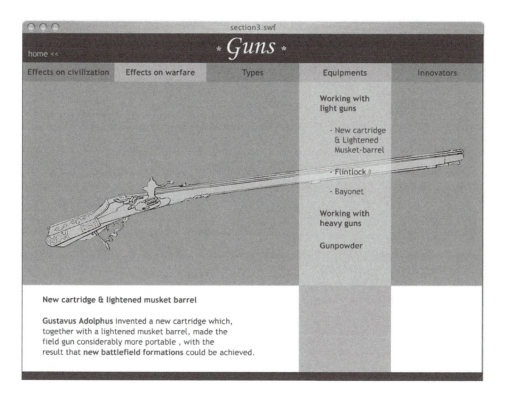

*Figure 4.4* Screen from 'guns' product by Alastair, Guy and Leslie

expression *new battlefield formations* to a page showing an image of these new battle-field formations. The text underneath the image partly repeats the text on the preceding screen and partly elaborates on it (see Figure 4.5).

So even explicit translations of network relations need some kind of textual realization, and the relation between the screens themselves is therefore one of 'expansion' – the page the link leads to *expands* the content of the emboldened wording on the previous screen. This seems to be the case not only with the links that translate network relations but also with those that translate other kinds of non-linear relations – trees, stars, etc. We will discuss this issue in more detail in Chapter 5.

So far we have discussed implicit and explicit translations of non-linear relations that are realized either only by textual grammatical relations or by textual grammatical relations and links leading to another screen. But the relations can also be realized by juxtaposing text and image, or image and an image–text combination. Whereas textual implicit realizations tend to be similar to those of the original linear text, in the case of juxtaposition realizations the semantic relation has to be inferred. An example is shown in Figure 4.6.

This screen is from an encyclopaedia of 'dangerous creatures' and concerns the

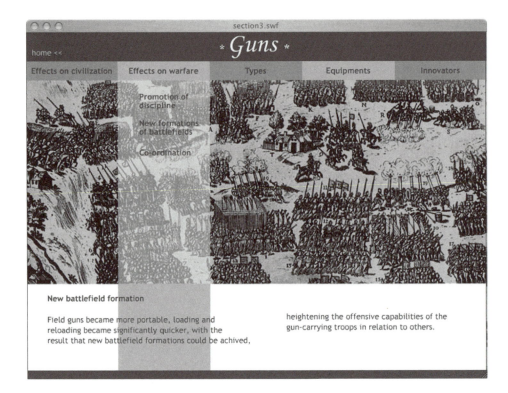

*Figure 4.5* Screen from 'guns' product by Alastair, Guy and Leslie

moray eel, more specifically its habit of hiding in holes. The top-right corner features a button with an image–text combination identifying a funnel-web spider. It leads to a screen dealing with this spider in more detail. The relation between the moray eel on the 'hiding in holes' page and the funnel-web spider in the navigation button is a network link that needs to be inferred and that could be worded, for instance, as 'also hides in holes' (which, indeed, is how the spider lives).

## Overt and covert translations

Explicit translations from non-linear models into some kind of perceivable design may be either overt or covert. In overt translations, the non-linear-model relations are iconically translated into a form that closely resembles the non-linear model itself. The overt translation of the star model, from Figure 3.15 in the previous chapter, is shown in Figure 4.7. The main component of the page is the star model itself, with *guns* as its nucleus, in the centre of the model, and *inventors, types, definitions* and *social effects* as its satellites, just as in the original model, but now in an

## Hiding in holes

Moray eels don't normally cruise around reefs, stalking their prey. Instead, they hide in holes among the rocks and coral. When a small fish or crab comes close, wham!— the eel suddenly darts out and grabs it with its sharp teeth. If a diver comes too close to a moray's hiding place, the eel may mistake a hand or foot for a fish.

*Figure 4.6* Screen from *Dangerous Creatures* (Microsoft, 1994)

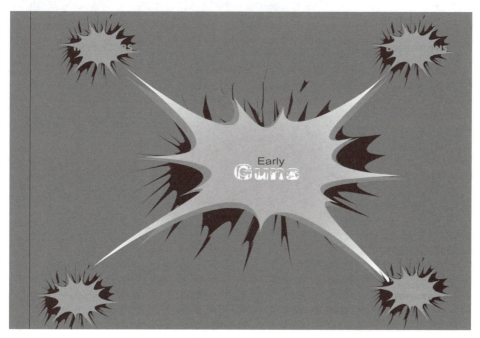

Early
Guns

*Figure 4.7* Jennifer, Kylie and Richard's 'guns' home page

aesthetically more attractive form. The satellites are clickable and lead to pages dealing with the satellites' topics in more detail.

Covert translations of non-linear models can be divided into different types. The main division is between translations into navigation and translations into interface. There are two ways of translating non-linear model relations into navigation – they can be translated either into a navigation device, or navigation bar, or into an underlined wording in a text. We have already seen examples of the latter. The translations into navigation devices result in various layouts of the navigation buttons in relation to each other, as well as in their positioning on the page. The most familiar navigation layout is the one that translates the tree model. The hierarchy between the nodes in the tree is represented by their position relative to one another, by their typeface and, at lower levels, by the indenting of the navigation buttons. The superordinate tree nodes, usually in a more prominent type, are above the subordinate nodes and at lower levels the subordinate nodes are indented. The section of a website page shown in Figure 4.8 is an example.

When non-linear models are translated into interfaces, the translation contributes to the interface design in a way that goes beyond the navigation buttons. There are three ways of doing this. The first is the use of headings that reflect the different non-linear models' levels, as shown in Figure 4.9, which translates the 'pendant/chatelaine' watch row of a table in the students' final non-linear diagram of the 'Art Deco

*Figure 4.8* Section of a page from the website of the Ohio Northern University

*Figure 4.9* Page from Christina, Rachel and Mohamed's 'Art Deco watches' product

watches' text. The headings (*gender, designers, decoration, dial* and *case*) translate the independent variables in the table, and the paragraphs that follow them provide detail about the form these variables can take.

Another way non-linear models can be covertly translated into interfaces is by means of other non-linear models. On the page shown in Figure 4.10, the superordinate of a tree (*types of guns*) is located in the Given, while one of four subordinates (*field artillery, arquebus, musket* and *two-man musket*) can be chosen as the New – *musket* was selected in this case. Polarizing the two levels of the tree structure in this way makes it possible to show both at the same time. Even while reading detailed information about the subordinates, the user can still see which superordinate they belong to. This group of students also translated the nucleus of the central star of their non-linear model as the main heading in the Given part of the interface and the satellites as the lower-level headings. The satellite headings are clickable and it is by clicking on them that the more detailed information about their subordinates appears in the New part of the interface.

Finally, non-linear models can be covertly translated into the interface as image processes of the type identified in Kress and van Leeuwen (2007). This kind of translation translates non-linear models into more familiar and less diagrammatic forms of visual representation. The relations remain as explicit as they are in non-linear models, but differently so, as the translation is covert. According to our view of new media design, the more explicitly the non-linear semantics of the original texts is

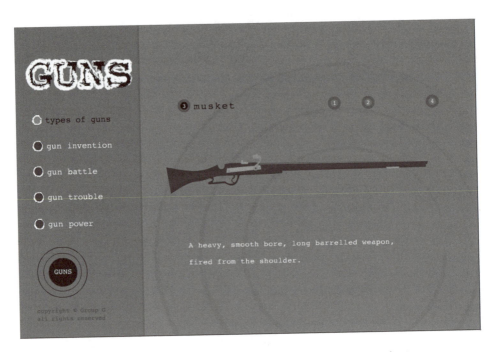

*Figure 4.10* Page from Alberto, Francisco and Morten's 'guns' product

represented, the better. There may of course come a point where one has to draw a line. Too much explicitness may make the translation too complex, and this may result in impaired usability. But generally speaking, explicit translations are better placed to take advantage of the non-linear and multimodal potential of the new media and result in better comprehension of the non-linear semantics of the original texts, and ultimately of the product itself.

The image process in the page shown in Figure 4.11 consists of the white circle containing the title *Inventors* and the three small images underneath it. It is a classificational process (Kress and van Leeuwen 2007) which visually translates the classification tree that formed part of the group's non-linear model of the 'guns' text. *Inventors* is the tree's superordinate and *The Chinese, Gustavus Adolphus* and *Maurice of Nassau* (all represented by images) are the subordinates. The images at the bottom of the tree also function as navigation buttons. When rolled over, they reveal short labels – *The Chinese, Gustavus Adolphus* and *Maurice of Nassau* – accompanied by the advice to *click for more information*. When a button is clicked on, a short text about the particular inventor appears in the bottom-left corner of the screen.

Clearly, there is a close relationship between the tree which this image process translates and the form of the image process itself. The classification relationship between the superordinate and the subordinates remains clear and explicit, but an aesthetic dimension is added by the font that realizes the superordinate, by the white

*Figure 4.11* Page from the 'guns' product of Jill, Anne and Veronica

circle that highlights the process, and by the images themselves. The image process thus contributes to the design of the interface. And the subordinates' images at the same time function as a navigation layer. In our opinion, this is a very successful translation of the tree, since it intertwines information architecture and interface design and makes good use of the medium's potential for multimodality and non-linearity.

The example also brings out the importance of the second translation. It is true that non-linear models of the kind we introduced in the previous chapters represent how we understand texts. If a new media product is based on a well-thought-out non-linear model that adequately represents the underlying semantic structure of a given text or domain, the product will be easier to understand and easier to use. At the same time, diagrams such as those we showed in Chapter 3 can be quite dense and fairly complex to read. They require familiarity with the diagrammatic conventions on which they are based, and lay users of new media products cannot necessarily be expected to possess this kind of diagrammatic 'literacy' (or 'graphicacy', as it is sometimes called; Roth *et al*. 2005). A good second translation therefore (1) on the one hand preserves the semantic structure of the diagram, but on the other hand expands the information, making it less dense, and (2) translates diagrammatic representation into forms of language, forms of visual communication and navigation devices with which the user is familiar. Provided our second translation rules are followed, new media products can represent non-linear semantics in ways that are engaging and easy to comprehend and do not require users to learn the conventions of reading diagrams (for the different ways images and text typically combine see Martinec and Salway 2005).

## Metaphorical translations

Our final kind of second translation involves the use of metaphor. Metaphors are of particular interest for new media design because they can combine creative and innovative expression with the verbal and visual realization of semantic structures. As for the former, Aristotle already knew it in the fourth century BC: 'Ordinary words convey only what we already know, it is from metaphor that we can best get hold of something new' (Aristotle 1954: 1410b), and poets have made creative use of metaphor throughout the centuries.

The essence of metaphor is the idea of 'transference', of transferring something from one place to another on the basis of a perceived analogy. Metaphor is also a multimodal concept, and visual metaphors are common in many types of images, for instance advertising images (Forceville 1996). But, according to Lakoff and Johnson (1980), metaphor is not only a source of new and vivid ways of expressing ideas, but also the basis of all human cognition. 'Structural metaphors' such as 'theories are buildings', they say, make it possible to say things like 'We've got the *framework* for a *well-constructed* argument', 'If you don't *support* your argument with *solid underpinnings*, the whole thing will *collapse*' and so on (Lakoff and Johnson 1980: 98). In other words, the structure of a building can become a vehicle for understanding the structure of theories. Note that such metaphors allow abstract entities and relations to be understood on the basis of concrete, observable entities and relations. This not only makes such abstract entities and relations easier to understand, it also makes it possible to illustrate them with images of concrete people, places and things. All this should make 'structural metaphors' a key tool for new media designers, provided the underlying analogies are relevant and well thought through.

We distinguish two kinds of metaphorical translation: translations involving the use of an image process and translations based on a narrative scenario. The latter need to be distinguished from simple introductions without a narrative element. We will give some examples of such introductions later, when discussing the various kinds of second translation in more detail.

An example of a metaphorical translation involving an image process is shown in Figure 4.12.

This is the home page of a student website that translates the 'guns' text. The students' star model was iconically translated into a shooting target, with the star's nucleus as the bull's eye and the satellites as hits spaced more or less symmetrically around it. In Kress and van Leeuwen's (2007) terms, it is an analytical process with *Guns* as the Carrier and the hits as the Attributes. The home page was preceded by a splash page with a short introduction, as represented in Figures 4.13 and 4.14.

*Figure 4.12* Home page from Alberto, Francisco and Morten's 'guns' product

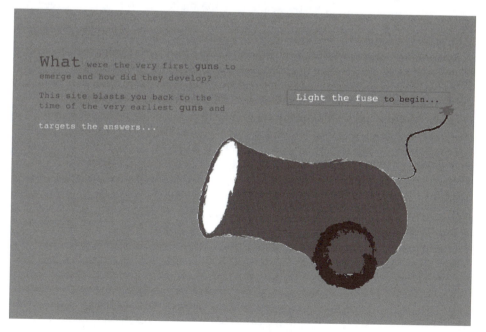

*Figure 4.13* Splash page from Alberto, Francisco and Morten's 'guns' product

*Figure 4.14* Splash page from Alberto, Francisco and Morten's 'guns' product

These splash pages *explain* the metaphor, making it clear that clicking on the 'shots' will lead users progressively closer to the bull's eye, the 'answer' they are 'targeting', just as Roget's Thesaurus leads its users progressively closer to the word that best expresses the idea they are seeking to express. In other words, through the metaphor of hitting a target the group tried to make the abstract process of information retrieval easier to understand, and easier to engage in.

The second type of metaphorical translation we will exemplify with a student website based on the 'Art Deco watches' text. The introductory page of the website is shown in Figure 4.15. It introduces 1920s Paris as an exciting playground for the bourgeois elite, but a more difficult place to survive in for others. Users are invited to identify with the latter and to settle the score by stealing expensive watches from rich citizens and selling them on the black market.

After clicking on the *Enter* sign, we hear the sound of a door opening and the scene changes to the interior of a typical Parisian café, populated with famous 1920s characters including Ernest Hemingway, Al Capone, Greta Garbo, Josephine Baker and others, as shown in Figure 4.16.

After clicking on one of the characters, he or she comes to the foreground and a dialogue box appears. The user can type a suitable introductory sentence in the box, e.g. 'Good evening', and elicit a reply by clicking on the *Chat* button. A speech bubble then appears next to the character, e.g. Al Capone answers the user's 'Good evening' with 'Hey man . . . wassup?'. As he is holding a cigar, the user may continue the conversation with 'Have you got a light?'. Clicking on the *Chat* button then produces Capone's reply: 'Sure buddy! So long as you ain't with that damned gendarmerie.'

*Figure 4.15* Introductory page of Norman, Lilie and Teun's 'Art Deco watches' product

*Figure 4.16* Parisian café (from Norman, Lilie and Teun's 'Art Deco watches' product)

A hand holding a lighter with an encased watch appears from the right and a pop-up window comes up with a description of the key attributes of the watch: *Lighter watch: gold, silver, platinum; dial hidden; Cartier, Boucheron* (see Figure 4.17).

The user can now type in something like 'What a nice lighter!'. Clicking on *Chat* will again bring up a reply from Capone: 'Sure is . . . and it also lets you know you've lived to see another day!' After a few similar exchanges with other characters in the café, a pop-up appears with a list of the watches shown so far and an instruction for users to select the one they want to steal. Ticking off one of the watches and clicking a button titled *Steal* results in a blacked-out screen and a sound of surprise and dismay, followed by footsteps fast disappearing in the distance and the sound of a police whistle.

Much of this narrative lingers on the image of 1920 Paris flâneurs and on the café with its famous habitués, translating – and expanding – the Given–New structure that introduced the 'Art Deco watches' text (cf. Figure 3.8). Information about the watches themselves is translated into the pop-ups by images of actual watches, their names and descriptions, and at times also into the dialogue itself. The metaphor suggests that information about such watches is something that comes about in a haphazard way, in the course of casual conversations, and something that must be obtained surreptitiously, stolen. Ingenuous and entertaining as this product may be, information about Art Deco watches becomes subservient here to a different agenda, driven by an interest in the period, rather than interest in watches. Users interested in finding information about Art Deco watches might find this website somewhat distracting and time-consuming.

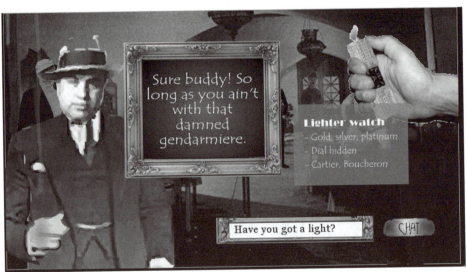

*Figure 4.17* Pop-up window with Art Deco watch attributes in Norman, Lilie and Teun's 'Art Deco watches' product

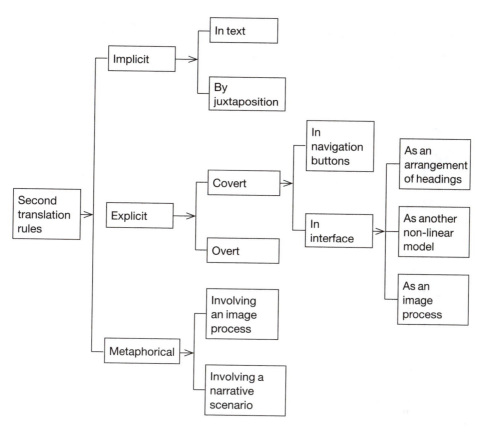

*Figure 4.18* Systematic representation of rules for translating non-linear models into navigation and interface ('second translation')

Figure 4.18 represents our 'second translation' rules that we have been discussing and exemplifying as a system of choices.

## Non-linear models and second translation rules

In this section, we will illustrate how our 'second translation' rules apply to each one of the non-linear models we presented in Chapter 2.

### Given–New and Ideal–Real

Figures 4.19 and 4.20 exemplify the implicit translation of Given–New structures in text.

The students who created this product had translated the introduction to the original 'Art Deco watches' text as the Given–New model shown in Figure 3.12 in the

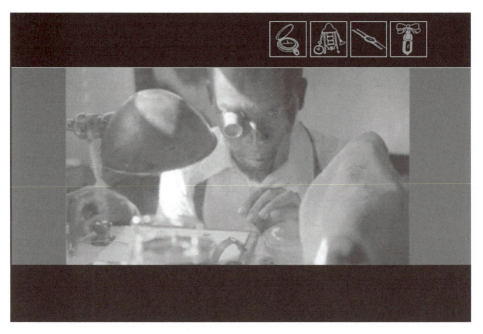

*Figure 4.19* Page from the 'Art Deco watches' product of Brogan, Philip and Janet

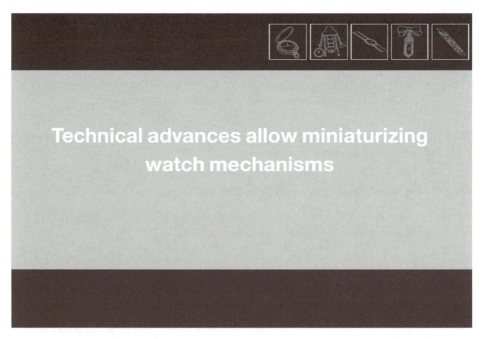

**Technical advances allow miniaturizing watch mechanisms**

*Figure 4.20* Page from the 'Art Deco watches' product of Brogan, Philip and Janet

previous chapter. In their second translation exemplified in Figures 4.19 and 4.20, the Given and New nodes were strung together in sentences that alternated with images that illustrated them. An image of a watchmaker working at his desk was followed by 'Technical advances allow miniaturizing watch mechanisms'; an image of a 1920s square milling with people was followed by 'In the 1920s people's lives became hectic and they became obsessed with time'; and so on. The succession of slow-moving images alternating with screens containing sentences of this kind introduced the main part of the site, where the different kinds of watches were compared.

Figure 4.21 exemplifies an implicit translation of Given and New by juxtaposition.

The Given–New relation is translated here into a juxtaposition of images expressing the theme of 'life in the fast lane' with speech bubbles popping up when the characters in the images are rolled over. An image of two women standing by a car is juxtaposed with the line 'I'll drink my tea in the car or else we will be late, let's hurry', to which the other woman replies 'Alright! Let's go . . . '; an image of a woman and a man standing in the garden of their villa is juxtaposed with the man's line 'It's already six o'clock', to which the woman replies 'Let's hurry, the dinner party starts at seven'; and so on. Other examples of Given–New relations are translated implicitly in text, by means of vignettes embedded in the scenes of fast life, e.g.: 'The leitmotif of the "Années Folles" was to live fast. The watch became an accessory of great importance.'

*Figure 4.21* Page from the 'Art Deco watches' product of Paul, Pirkko and Devleena

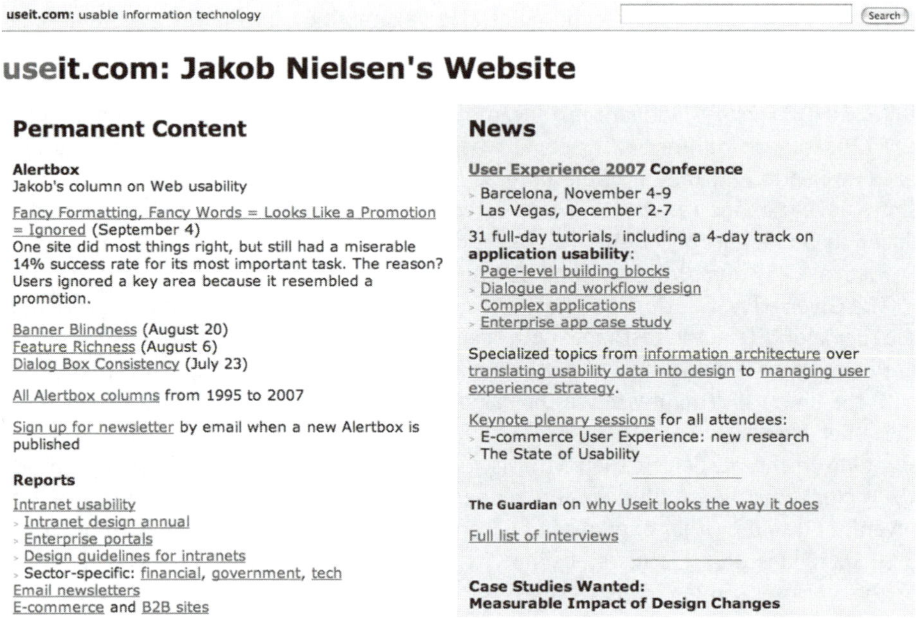

*Figure 4.22* Section of a page from Jakob Nielsen's website

Figure 4.22 provides an example of an overt translation of the Given–New structure.

Unsurprisingly, there do not seem to be any covert or metaphorical translations of the Given–New model. The model consists of pairs of contrasting concepts, so it would not make much sense to translate it by means of a star, a tree or another non-linear model. Translating it into navigation buttons or as an arrangement of headings does not seem to make much sense either because there are usually more than two of these. As for second translations of the Ideal–Real model, we have not come across any at all, most probably for much the same reasons that are behind the scarcity of Given–New translations.

## The star

We have already given several examples of overt and covert star translations. We will now discuss all the translation options following our system of second translation rules. Figures 4.23 and 4.24 provide two implicit translations, both based on the non-linear model shown in Figure 4.25.

The star relations translated into these pages are between *polyphony* and *melodic independence* on the one hand, and between *polyphony* and *rhythmic independence* on the other. The first of the two, the relation between *polyphony* and *melodic independence*, is translated into the text of the interface as 'One of the two essential

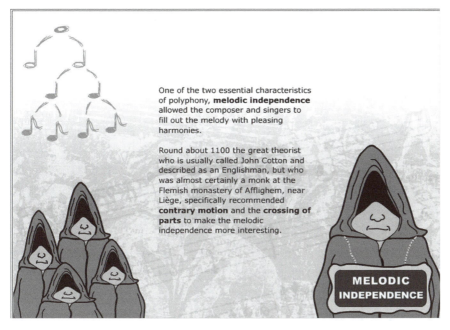

One of the two essential characteristics of polyphony, **melodic independence** allowed the composer and singers to fill out the melody with pleasing harmonies.

Round about 1100 the great theorist who is usually called John Cotton and described as an Englishman, but who was almost certainly a monk at the Flemish monastery of Afflighem, near Liège, specifically recommended **contrary motion** and the **crossing of parts** to make the melodic independence more interesting.

MELODIC INDEPENDENCE

*Figure 4.23* Page from Will, Sue and Katy's 'polyphonic music' product

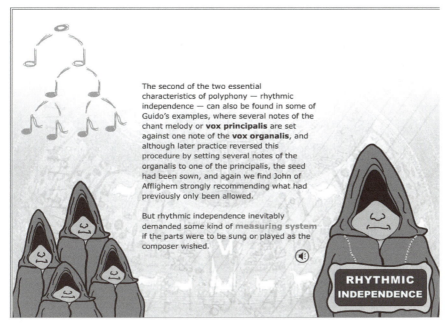

The second of the two essential characteristics of polyphony — rhythmic independence — can also be found in some of Guido's examples, where several notes of the chant melody or **vox principalis** are set against one note of the **vox organalis**, and although later practice reversed this procedure by setting several notes of the organalis to one of the principalis, the seed had been sown, and again we find John of Afflighem strongly recommending what had previously only been allowed.

But rhythmic independence inevitably demanded some kind of measuring system if the parts were to be sung or played as the composer wished.

RHYTHMIC INDEPENDENCE

*Figure 4.24* Page from Will, Sue and Katy's 'polyphonic music' product

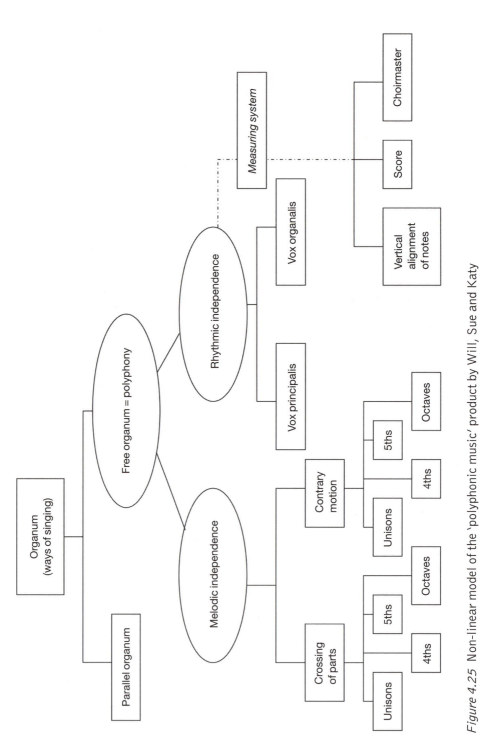

*Figure 4.25* Non-linear model of the 'polyphonic music' product by Will, Sue and Katy

characteristics of polyphony, melodic independence, allowed the composer and singers to fill out the melody with pleasing harmonies' (Figure 4.23). The second of the two relations, between *polyphony* and *rhythmic independence*, is translated into 'The second of the two essential characteristics of polyphony – rhythmic independence – can also be found in some of Guido's examples' (Figure 4.24).

Translating star relations by juxtaposition is probably impossible. The reason is that this kind of translation can only work for non-linear models in which the nodes are related by equal relations. In such cases, the content of the different nodes is in principle independent, which may result in the need for inferring the content of one node from the content of the other. The nodes in the star model, however, are not independent – in fact, it is part of the definition of the star model that the satellites are dependent on the nucleus.

There are many examples of overt translations of stars in our students' products. Most of our students in fact translated the main level of their non-linear models of the 'guns' text into an overt star. The nucleus in this case tended to be realized by an image with 'guns' as the title, and the satellites were realized similarly. We already discussed the example shown in Figure 4.7, in which the satellites function as naviga-tion buttons, taking the user to the next layer of the product's structure. Despite this, we see all overt translations as translations into the interface because if overt transla-tions are to be usable as navigation devices, they have to be over a certain size, and once that happens, they make an often quite significant contribution to the look of the interface. It is quite impossible for an overt star or tree or any other model to occupy the small amount of space that navigation devices usually do, and yet enable the user to click reliably and comfortably on the nodes in order to get to the other layers of the product's structure. The overt translation of the 'guns' star model in Figure 4.26 is a good example. The revolver drum-like navigation device in the top-left corner of the screen is large enough to be usable and to also make a contribution to the look of the interface. If we take the labels of the navigation buttons into account as well, the whole device is in fact bigger than the text below it.

An example of a covert translation into navigation of the star in a non-linear model of the 'guns' text is shown in Figure 4.27.

While the nucleus is not clickable and only provides a unifying title for the satel-lites, the satellites themselves are translated into an unordered row of navigation buttons below the nucleus. In the case of this product, the buttons do not lead to screens at the next layer of structure. They only function as superordinates of the navigation buttons below them, which translate the subordinate nodes of the trees that join the satellite nodes in the non-linear model (which is shown in Figure 3.17). Just as in the complex non-linear model, in this navigation scheme, too, the first-level star's satellites become the second-level tree's superordinates.

Although not very common, the above translation of a star nucleus as a heading at the top of a screen and of its satellites as a row of navigation buttons below it seems to be an accepted second translation in web design. Figure 4.28 shows an example of an existing website that uses this pattern.

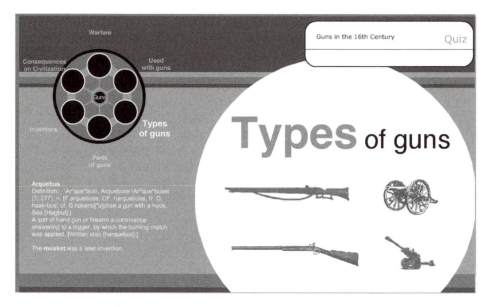

*Figure 4.26* Page from Jill, Anne and Veronica's 'guns' product

*Figure 4.27* Home page from Alastair, Guy and Leslie's 'guns' product

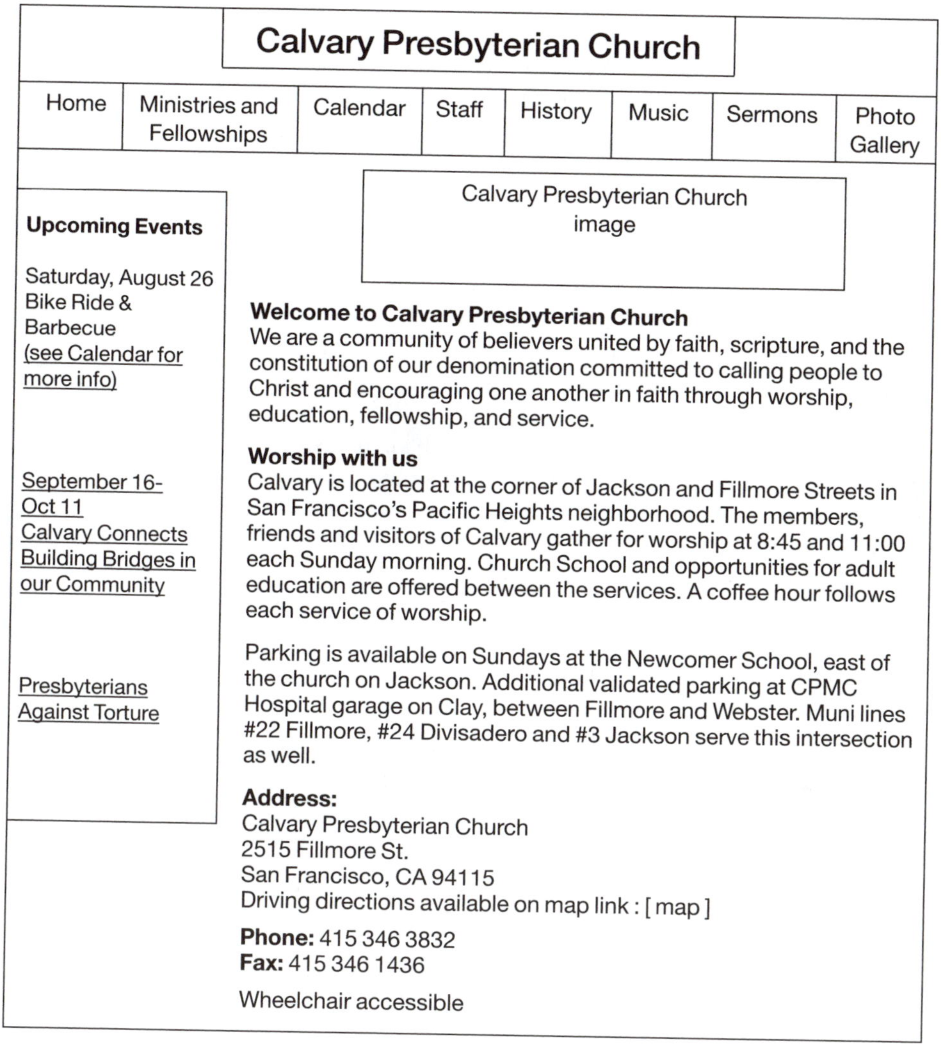

| Calvary Presbyterian Church | | | | | | | |
|---|---|---|---|---|---|---|---|
| Home | Ministries and Fellowships | Calendar | Staff | History | Music | Sermons | Photo Gallery |

**Upcoming Events**

Saturday, August 26
Bike Ride &
Barbecue
(see Calendar for
more info)

September 16-
Oct 11
Calvary Connects
Building Bridges in
our Community

Presbyterians
Against Torture

Calvary Presbyterian Church
image

**Welcome to Calvary Presbyterian Church**
We are a community of believers united by faith, scripture, and the constitution of our denomination committed to calling people to Christ and encouraging one another in faith through worship, education, fellowship, and service.

**Worship with us**
Calvary is located at the corner of Jackson and Fillmore Streets in San Francisco's Pacific Heights neighborhood. The members, friends and visitors of Calvary gather for worship at 8:45 and 11:00 each Sunday morning. Church School and opportunities for adult education are offered between the services. A coffee hour follows each service of worship.

Parking is available on Sundays at the Newcomer School, east of the church on Jackson. Additional validated parking at CPMC Hospital garage on Clay, between Fillmore and Webster. Muni lines #22 Fillmore, #24 Divisadero and #3 Jackson serve this intersection as well.

**Address:**
Calvary Presbyterian Church
2515 Fillmore St.
San Francisco, CA 94115
Driving directions available on map link : [ map ]

**Phone:** 415 346 3832
**Fax:** 415 346 1436

Wheelchair accessible

*Figure 4.28* Drawing after the home page of Calvary Presbyterian Church website

*Calvary Presbyterian Church* is the main topic of this website and the first-layer navigation buttons represent smaller semantic fields, all of which are related to, or are attributes of, the Calvary Presbyterian Church. The non-linear model behind this navigation design is thus the star.

Another way of covertly translating a star into navigation is by horizontal navigation buttons at the bottom-right position of a screen. While the previous translation is especially suited to the top navigation layer, this one is best for lower layers. The reason is that, in much existing design, the higher layer(s) are represented either by a tracking bar at the top of the page or by a covert tree in the top-left corner. We consider the bottom-right corner to be the preferred position for navigation bars that translate star patterns at lower layers since they are clearly set apart from both the tracking bar at the top of the page and the covert tree in the top-left corner. We did not find instances of this covert translation of a star into navigation on the web or in other new media products. The web is so vast that this of course does not mean this kind of translation does not exist. But even if it did not, we believe it should become a new media convention since the bottom-right corner position has generally not been exploited for navigation and since it does set the navigation bar clearly apart as a covert star translation. Figure 4.29, which translates the two star relations from the 'polyphonic music' non-linear model (see Figure 3.1), presents an example of such a navigation bar.

The title of the page is *Free Organum* and the page explains what it is. The explanation is in our opinion not very clear and the page lacks an outline of the topics at the next layer of structure. It is thus a good idea for the two star navigation buttons – *Rhythmic independence* and *Melodic independence* – to be labelled *Characteristics*, which indicates that the two kinds of independence are attributes of the *Free Organum*. The label would not have been necessary had the relationship been clarified in the text. Clicking on the navigation buttons leads to pop-up windows with a description and an illustration of rhythmic and melodic independence by both sound and an animated note staff.

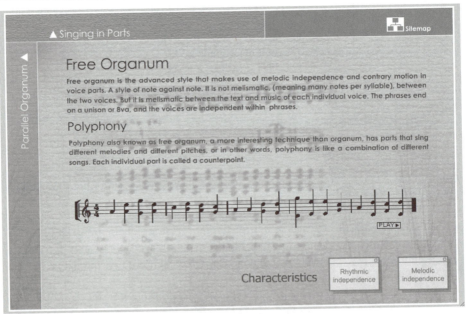

*Figure 4.29* Screen from the 'polyphonic music' product of Regina, Janneke and Ping

We will now discuss covert translations of the star model into interface. First of all, we have not been able to identify any examples of translations of the star as an arrangement of headings that would be specific to the star model. There does not seem to be a convention for such a translation in the old media and, if it does at all exist in new media, it must be infrequent. One can imagine that such a translation, if it did exist, would follow the conventions for translating a tree, as in the following example, where *Polyphony* is translated as the main heading and *Melodic independence* and *Rhythmic independence* as subordinate ones (see Figure 4.30).

Figure 4.31 is an example of a covert star translated into an image process. The Michelangelo hand, with its three blobs of light emanating from the fingers and its attached labels, is an analytical process (see Kress and van Leeuwen 2007). The three blobs of light and their labels are the Attributes and the hand is their Carrier. The Attributes function as navigation buttons that take the user to the next layer of the product's structure where the topics are treated in more detail. Analytical processes are the obvious choice for translating stars because they consist of Carriers and Attributes. The Carriers translate the star's nuclei and the Attributes the star's satellites. The same kind of attributive relations underlie both analytical processes and stars.

Figure 4.31 can also be seen as the translation of a star by the Ideal–Real model. The nucleus of the star (*guns*) is at the bottom of the screen, and so represents the Real, whereas the satellites are in the top half, as the Ideal. This is a rather unusual translation, as one would expect the nucleus to be translated as the Ideal and the

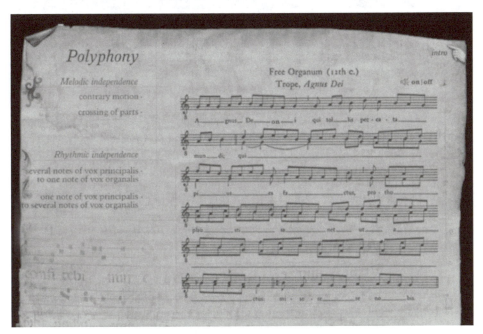

*Figure 4.30* Page from the 'polyphonic music' product of Harry, Froukje and Emily

*Figure 4.31* Page from the 'guns' product of Gunther, Terry and Jim

satellites as the Real. But in this case the motivation comes from the satellites being part of the image of the hand, whereas the nucleus is simply translated as text (*guns*). As we have seen in Figure 2.10, when images and text realize the Ideal–Real model, the images generally function as the Ideal and the text as the Real.

One more example of the star translated as another non-linear model is the Given–New structure shown in Figure 4.32.

We think this can be seen as a translation of a star into interface because, although the headings in the alphabetically ordered list of translations of 'Gateway to the European Union' in the member states' languages function as navigation buttons, there is nothing apart from them and the nucleus (*Europa*) to make up the interface. The Given–New arrangement of the nucleus and the satellites thus *is* this interface.

An example of a metaphorical translation of the star model is represented in Figure 4.33.

The students who made this product chose to translate the 'Art Deco watches' text by a star rather than a table (see Figure 3.9). Their second translation was quite creative, using the metaphor of a watch shop. Yet it remained strongly motivated by the star model itself. Clicking on the manufacturers' names on the board in the front-right corner brings up information about the manufacturers in the bottom-right corner of the screen, illustrated by example watches. It also makes a speech bubble

**Europa**

| | |
|---|---|
| cs | Portál Evropské unie |
| da | Internetportalen til EU |
| de | Das Portal der Europäischen Union |
| et | Euroopa Liidu portaal |
| el | Η δικτυακ? π?λη της Ευρωπα?κ?ς ?νο |
| en | Gateway to the European Union |
| es | El portal de la Unión Europea |
| fr | Le portail de l'Union européenne |
| it | Il portale dell'Unione europea |
| lv | Eiropas Savieni˜bas porta˜ls |
| lt | Europos Sa jungos portalas |
| hu | Az Európai Unió portálja |
| mt | Il-portal ta' l-Unjoni Ewropea |
| nl | De portaalsite van de Europese Unie |
| pl | Portal Unii Europejskiej |
| pt | O portal da União Europeia |
| sk | Portál Európskej únie |
| sl | Portal Evropske unije |
| fi | Euroopan unionin portaali |
| sv | EU:s webbportal |

*Figure 4.32* Section of European Union website page

*Figure 4.33* Home page of the 'Art Deco watches' product of Maryam, Jane and Rirette

with further information emerge from the shop owner's mouth. Clicking on the watches in the display case at the back of the shop makes another speech bubble appear: 'An inventive richness went into the design not only of *ladies'* watches, but also of *men's*.' Clicking either on *ladies'* or *men's* brings up speech bubbles with information about different kinds of women's and men's watches and makes images of these watches appear in the bottom-right corner. Clicking on the large mechanism of a clock in front of the shop assistant brings up a speech bubble containing information about the advances in watchmaking that enabled the miniaturization of watches, as well as an illustration of watch mechanisms in the bottom-right corner. Clicking on the billiard balls on the left of the clock makes another speech bubble appear with a description of the materials used in making the watches. At the same time, examples of watches made of the materials appear in the bottom-right corner. In other words, each of the satellites of the star is thus metaphorically represented by one of these objects. All of them taken together create a circle around the shop assistant who is in the centre, which makes the design mirror the structure of the star model, with its central nucleus surrounded by satellites.

### The tree

Let us now turn to the second translation of the tree. Overt translations of trees into either interface or navigation do not seem to have taken hold in new media, and they are rare in print as well. Covert trees, however, are probably the most common second translation of all, especially in the form of website navigation menus in the top-left corner of screens. But they do not always realize semantic relations in the way we have recommended and may, instead, be used in the same manner as the tables of contents are used in books, to show the contents of the various layers of structure: the 'chapters', 'sections' and 'subsections' of websites and other new media products. Some of these websites, e.g. the ShopNike.com website we will analyse and redesign in Chapter 6, have trees with a large number of layers. But these trees mix purely semantic relations with relations that are neither classification nor composition relations but simply inclusions in the physical, or formal, sense of the word.

To ascertain whether a navigation tree reflects the semantics of a new media product's contents, it is necessary to analyse the content of the pages that are related by the navigation buttons. We believe that the best designs have navigation structures that reflect the semantic structure of the new media product's content. When this is the case, the structure of the product, with all its various layers and inter-relationships, articulates the content optimally by making the relationships between the various content parts explicit and so helping the user process the content most efficiently. Less satisfactory matches between the content's semantic structure and the structure of the navigation result in less than optimal understanding. We will first discuss the different kinds of tree translations and later move on to an example of an existing website in which the covert navigation trees are trees in only the formal sense of physical inclusion.

The implicit translation of a tree into text is common in both new and old media. An example from one of our students' projects is shown in Figure 4.34. The page implicitly translates a tree that has *melodic independence* as its superordinate and *contrary motion* and *crossing of parts* as its subordinates into the following text: 'To make a piece of music melodically independent, the composer can make use of various stylistic elements. These include "contrary motion" and the "crossing of parts".'

We cannot show examples of the implicit translation of tree relationships into juxtapositions since, as we have explained, this kind of translation only applies to non-linear models whose nodes are of equal status, and the tree is not one of these.

As for overt tree translations, the only example that occurred in our students' work is in Figure 4.35.

This product opened with the tree that formed the main component of the complex non-linear model extracted from the 'music' text, namely the division of organa (singing in parts) into free organum and parallel organum. Clicking on *free organum* makes *parallel organum* recede in the background and the two attributes of *melodic independence* and *rhythmic independence* appear below free organum. Clicking on either makes an animated note staff appear where the attributes are demonstrated to

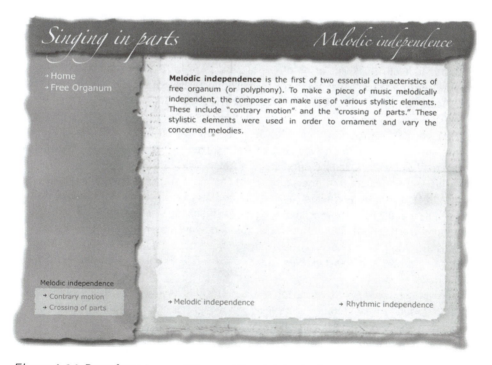

*Figure 4.34* Page from Laura, Pilar and Bessie's 'polyphonic music' product

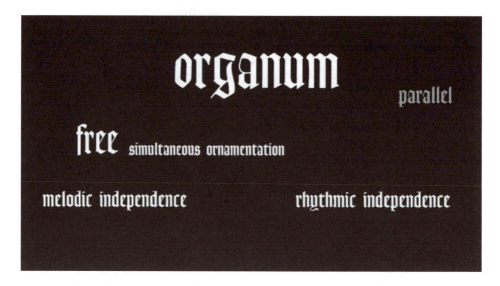

*Figure 4.35* Page from Terry, Will and Jon's 'polyphonic music' product

the tune of appropriate recordings. The translation is not particularly successful, since translating the tree overtly by simply repeating the tree's labels and their layout does not make a great use of the new media potential for either multimodality or non-linearity. As well, the translation of the attributes of the free organum, or rather of the star relations that link them to the free organum, are not sufficiently distinct from the translation of the tree relations that link free organum and parallel organum to organum.

The covert translation of tree relations into navigation buttons is, as we already mentioned, a very common way of translating trees. Figure 4.36 (which we also showed as Figure 4.27) is an example.

In this second translation, the satellites of the main star in the complex non-linear model are translated as navigation buttons making up a horizontal navigation bar and simultaneously function as superordinates of second-level trees which are trans-lated into the vertical navigation bars going downwards from the horizontal bar buttons. Clicking on the covertly translated subordinates, such as *Arquebus, Musket, Two-man musket* and *Field artillery*, takes the user to the pages that deal with these topics in detail.

An example of a covert translation of tree relations as an arrangement of headings is in the screen represented in Figure 4.37 (shown previously as Figure 4.2).

In this translation, a composition tree from the non-linear diagram created by this group of students was translated as an arrangement of headings followed by para-graphs that developed the subordinate topics. *Later musket*, which was the tree's superordinate, stands out by being in prominent font and by being positioned higher

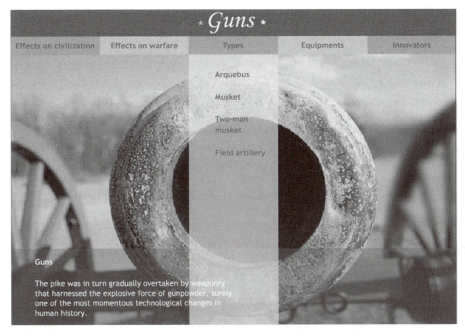

*Figure 4.36* Page from the 'guns' product of Alastair, Guy and Leslie

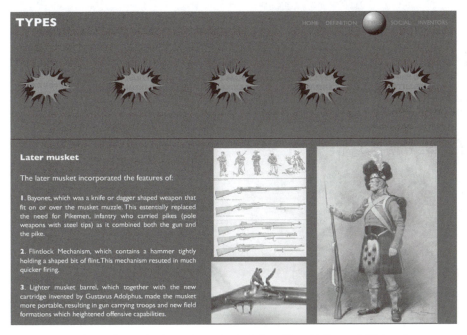

*Figure 4.37* Page from the 'guns' product of Jennifer, Kylie and Richard

on the page, whereas the subordinates are numbered and in less prominent font, with the paragraphs they head divided by equal spacing.

Trees can also be translated into other non-linear models such as Given–New and Ideal–Real. An example of a translation into Given–New is shown in Figure 4.38.

This group of students decided to translate the 'watches' text as a tree rather than a table (see Figure 3.10). They used the metaphor of a shady character selling cheap copies of the different types of watches in front of the College of Printing. When the user clicks on him, he grows in size and opens his coat. On the left side of the coat's lining are men's watches and on the right women's. The Given–New polarization is thus used to translate the main division in the students' tree, the division between men's and women's watches. Clicking on one of the watches leads to a screen with a close-up of the character's hand holding the watch, a voice bubble and a tag describing the characteristics of the watch.

A good example of the covert translation of a tree into an image process was shown in Figure 4.11. The tree in that example was a classificational tree, while that in Figure 4.39 is a compositional tree. The example is from the *Rough Guide* guide-books website and it is the home page of a guide to the USA. The non-linear model that can be extracted from this site is a compositional tree, as shown in Figure 4.40.

The interface in Figure 4.39 consists of an analytical image process (Kress and van

*Figure 4.38* Screen from the 'Art Deco watches' product of Rudi, Rigel and John

*Figure 4.39* Map from the Rough Guide to the USA website

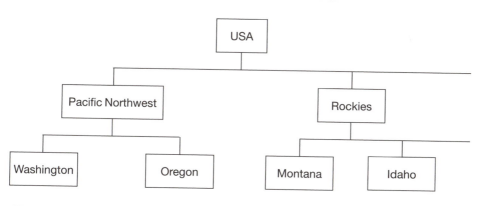

*Figure 4.40* Compositional tree representing the semantic structure of Figure 4.39

Leeuwen 2007), with the USA as the Carrier and its regions (represented by boundaries, different colours, and labels such as *California, Pacific Northwest, Southwest*)
as the Attributes. The compositional relationships between the different regions and
the various states that make them up are represented as covert navigation trees.

A metaphorical translation of a tree is the board with the names of the watchmakers in the watch shop we already featured in Figure 4.33. The *Manufacturers*
heading at the top of the board and the list of the manufacturers underneath it are

similar to a translation by an arrangement of headings. What makes this translation metaphorical is its use as part of the notice board advertising the *Live Fast* collection of watches in the shop.

We have mentioned that many of the covert trees that function as navigation devices on existing internet websites are a mixture of genuinely semantic trees and trees based simply on the principle of physical inclusion. Let us take a look at an example website where navigation both follows and flouts the semantic structure of its content. The site provides information on building websites for charity fundraising (http://mysite.wanadoo-members.co.uk/hitdonate/index.html). Figure 4.41 shows a page from this website that is a good example of how, according to our approach, the semantic structure of the content should correlate with the navigation.

**hitdonate.net**

website design for fundraising    about hitdonate    join email list    design and consultancy

Home > Online Fundraising Today > Underperforming

Homepage
Online fundraising today

Online fundraising today: a summary

► Why is the sector underperforming?

Poor online presence

Poor user experience

Insufficient trust

Do people prefer donating offline?

Emotional linkage

Sites that work
User experience
Building trust
Designing content
Asking for money
Repeat visitors
Streamlining the process
Donor Relationship
Everything else

## Why is the sector underperforming?

**So despite the potential for charities to have won new audiences and new sources of funds online, the majority do not seem to have done so. Why?**

Why do so many more people donate off-line rather than online, even though they have the means and the willingness to donate online?

There are several possible explanations that seem to be worth exploring, all of which are explored in more detail in the rest of this manual but are here as a quick summary if you lack the time or inclination to wade through the rest of this thing.

- Because charities have a **poor web presence**, or insufficient numbers of people are visiting charity sites
- Because charities online are failing to provide a **good user experience**
- Because web users lack sufficient **trust** in the charity or in the process of online donations
- People **prefer** donating offline
- There seems little or no **emotional linkage** or loyalty to most charities online

Join Cybergifts discussion list

Join Fundraising UK discussion list

**Next page
Poor online presence**

*Figure 4.41* 'Five reasons' page from a charity fundraising website

- Because charities have a poor web presence or insufficient numbers of people are visiting charity sites
- Because charities online are failing to provide a good user experience
- Because web users lack sufficient trust in the charity or in the process of online donations
- People prefer donating offline
- There seems little or no emotional linkage or loyalty to most charities online.

In terms of our system of second translation rules, this translates a classification tree which has the *reasons why the sector is underperforming* as its superordinate and the five reasons themselves as its subordinates. The navigation buttons then condense these subordinates into *Poor online presence, Poor user experience, Insufficient trust, Do people prefer donating offline?* and *Emotional linkage.* The line *Why is the sector underperforming?* is placed above them as a superordinate. On clicking, each subordinate node expands into a page with a more detailed explanation of the relevant reason at the next layer of the website's structure. The way the classification tree is translated into navigation thus mirrors the implicitly realized classification tree in the text of this page.

Compare this with the page reproduced in Figure 4.42.

The page is titled 'Online Fundraising Today: A summary of facts and figures' and it 'brings together some of the available figures on onsite fundraising, as at the end of summer 2000'. The navigation button corresponding to this content is *Online fundraising today: a summary.* It is presented as if it was a superordinate of *Main themes* and *The potential,* in exactly the same layout as the page shown in Figure 4.41. But the semantic relationship between the superordinate node and the subordinate nodes is completely different here, and there is no condensation relationship between the main text and the navigation buttons.

A (very faintly) highlighted network link from this page ('The *next page* is an attempt to pull a few themes together from these figures') leads to another page where the themes are discussed. We agree that the relationship between this page and the 'themes' page is a network link and that the accepted design convention is a highlighted (or underlined) piece of text. But the same network relationship is represented as if it was a tree in the arrangement of the navigation buttons. This can only lead to confusion.

The relationship between the content of the 'Online Fundraising Today: A summary of facts and figures' page and the 'The Potential' page, and therefore the corresponding *Online fundraising today: a summary* navigation button and the *The potential* button, is not a tree relationship either. While the 'Online Fundraising Today: A summary of facts and figures' page brings together some of the available figures on online fundraising, the 'The Potential' page outlines the intersection between the

**Home > Online Fundraising Today**

## Online Fundraising Today:
## A summary of facts and figures

**This page brings together some of the available figures on onsite fundraising, as at the end of summer 2000.**

I've concentrated on onsite fundraising here, although charities do have at their disposal other important sources of online income such as via charity shopping malls, donation portals and online charity auctions (summarized in Section 10). The next page is an attempt to pull a few themes together from these figures.

### American Lung Association
Raises $200,000 a year through its website (plus a 'minimal' amount of income received through donation portals). *(Source: C3 - see bottom of page for key)*

### American Red Cross
*International aid*
Raised $2.7 million online during 1999, compared to $817 million in total donations (0.33%) (C2). In the period July 1996 and April 1998, the organization received 1004 online donations for a total of $128,074. (Johnston)

### America's Second Harvest
*Food-bank network*
Raised $36,586 through 220 donations to its website between November 29 and December 31 1999. This was up from 70 gifts totalling $9125 in the same period in

**Other fundraising methods**
(donation portals, charity malls, ISPs, micro-payments)

**Next page**
**Main themes**

*Figure 4.42* 'Fundraising today' page from a charity fundraising website

online and charitable environments, and looks at the audiences already open to charities online. The *Online fundraising today: a summary*, *Main themes* and *The potential* buttons should thus not be part of the covert navigation tree, but should form an alternative navigation scheme of their own. In Chapter 6 we will redesign some other websites to show how this can be done.

## *The table*

Tables are about comparison and their translation should preserve that meaning. An example of the implicit translation into text of a table from a non-linear diagram based on the 'Art Deco watches' text is shown in Figure 4.43.

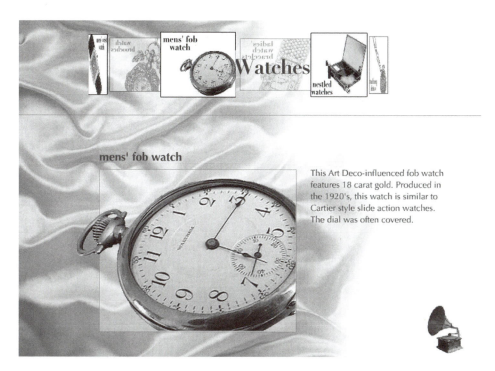

mens' fob watch

This Art Deco-influenced fob watch features 18 carat gold. Produced in the 1920's, this watch is similar to Cartier style slide action watches. The dial was often covered.

*Figure 4.43* Fob watch screen from Sarah, David and Betsy's 'Art Deco watches' product

The text compares the Art Deco-influenced fob watch displayed in the image with Cartier-style slide action watches. It is an implicit translation of the table into text because there is no hint of the table form, as there would be in an overt translation, nor is there any other graphic that would suggest some other kind of covert translation.

Tables lend themselves well to implicit juxtaposition translations, since the independent variables are equal in status, so that comparison can be achieved by juxtaposing the relevant attributes. We are not saying that this is necessarily the best way to compare things since users may have to work quite hard to spot the attributes that are being compared, but it is certainly a possibility, as exemplified by Figure 4.44.

In this example, the two kinds of watches are compared in terms of material (gold in the case of the shuttered watch and gold, enamel, diamonds and precious stones in the case of the bracelet watch), and design (Cartier vs Maisons). The text in both cases, however, reads like a description and the meaning of comparison is not made explicit and has to be inferred by the user. Figure 4.44 is also an example of translation into another non-linear model, since one of the two implicitly compared watches appears in the Given and the other in the New position. The website used this template to compare the other watch types as well.

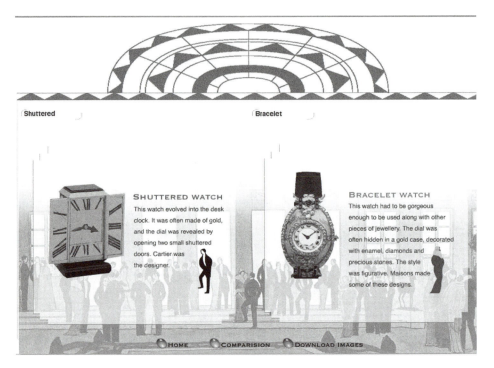

*Figure 4.44* Screen from Stefan, Adam and Julia's 'Art Deco watches' product

Overt translations of tables are also possible. One student group translated the part of the 'guns' text that explained the different types of guns and their characteristics into a table that also included the periods during which the different types of guns were current. In their interpretation of this part of the text they therefore focused on comparing the guns. Again, we are not saying that this is necessarily the best translation of that part of the table, but the overt translation is nevertheless quite interesting. Figure 4.46 shows the translation, and Figure 4.45 the table on which it was based.

The table in Figure 4.46 is three-dimensional, the three axes consisting of the independent variable (the types of guns) and the two dependent ones (their features and periods). The three variables intersect in particular cells of the table. Clicking on *two-man musket*, for instance, brings up a pop-up window looking like a ray of light, in which a description of the two-man musket appears, together with an image of the musket being fired from a forked rest. The same pop-up appears when *forked rest* is clicked on, and again when clicking on *mid-16th century*. The third dependent variable, efficacy, also appears in the pop-up.

When translating tables into navigation, the independent variables from the first column of the table are usually translated as the first navigation layer of the product and one of the attributes may then be translated as forming the second layer of navigation, as for instance in Figure 4.47.

| Type | Features | Efficiency | Period |
|---|---|---|---|
| Arquebus | Ten-pound, four-foot | | In the wars (Spain and Italy) |
| Musket | Fifteen-pound, six-foot | | By the middle of the 16th century |
| Two-man musket | A forked rest, two-ounce ball | Penetrate all armour, some three hundred yards range | |
| Gustavus' gun | A cartridge | More portable, quicker loading and reloading. More offensive capabilities | The absolutist period |
| Later development of guns | A flintlock | Augmented the rate of fire | |
| | A bayonet | Guns used as pike as well | After that . . . |

*Figure 4.45* Tabular representation of part of the 'guns' text by Gunther, Terry and Jim

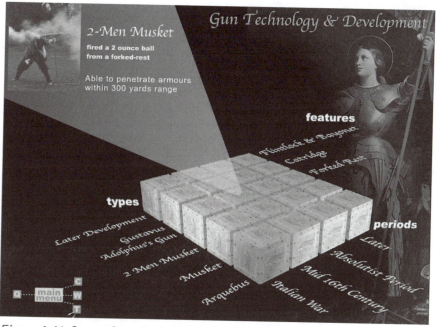

*Figure 4.46* Screen from the 'guns' product of Gunther, Terry and Jim, based on the table in Figure 4.45

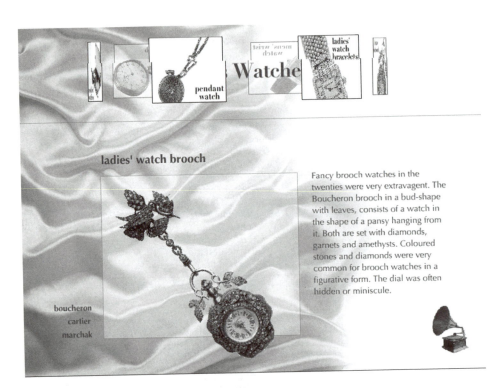

*Figure 4.47* Screen from the 'Art Deco watches' product of Sarah, David and Betsy

The first layer of navigation is formed here by the moving ring formed by the images of different types of watches at the top of the screen. Clicking on any one of them brings up the image and the text in the main part of the screen. Each watch type also varies according to its manufacturer and this forms a second layer of navigation realized by the navigation buttons in the bottom-left corner (*boucheron, cartier, marchak*) and leading to the appearance of the relevant images and text in the main part of the page.

Let us now turn to the translation of tables into arrangements of headings. An example of this is shown in Figure 4.48.

The pattern in the main part of the screen consists of an image, the independent variable (i.e. the watch types, displayed as a title on the right), and the dependent variables (i.e. the watch attributes, displayed as an arrangement of headings on the left). Each heading is followed by a paragraph describing the particular attribute for the watch type that is currently displayed. The Given–New model is used as well, to translate the two main axes of the model, i.e. the independent and dependent variables. In our opinion, it would have been better to place the watch types on the left and their attributes on the right. This would have preserved the left–right order of the columns in the table. The more 'natural', or iconic, the second translation, the better

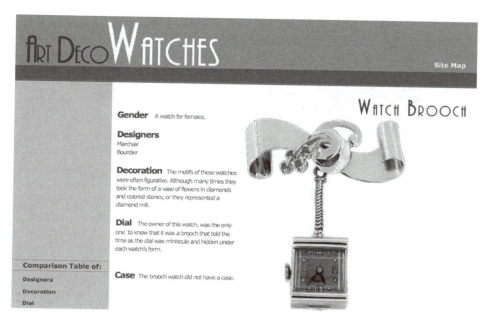

Figure 4.48 Screen from the 'Art Deco watches' product of Christina, Rachel and Mohamed

chance the user has to understand the non-linear semantics of the new media product. This principle, the principle of the natural relation between meaning and form, underlies the way semiotic systems work generally, including the relationship between the semantics and grammar of language (see Halliday 1994), and it is therefore of fundamental importance for effective new media design.

A rather successful translation of the 'watches' table by an image process is exemplified in Figure 4.49.

The first navigation layer is formed here by the independent variables (i.e. the watch types), as tends to be the norm. It takes the form of a horizontal bar made up of image buttons. Clicking on each of them results in the appearance of a window with an image of the watch and its parts (the dial, the casing, the strap, etc.). There is a small navigation menu in the top-right corner of the window, made up of the watch attributes (materials, decoration, form, dial, manufacturer, watchcase and the sex of the wearer). Rolling over each kind of attribute makes a particular value appear for the watch that is currently displayed. For example, rolling over *decoration* makes *Art Deco* appear. The image in the window is an analytical process, with the watch as a whole as the Carrier and the parts as its Attributes (see Kress and van Leeuwen 2007).

We have already seen one metaphorical translation of the 'watches' table involving a narrative scenario in Figures 4.16 and 4.17. In Figure 4.50 we present an example that involves an image process.

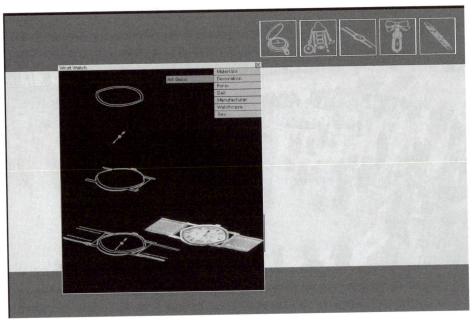

*Figure 4.49* Screen from Brogan, Philip and Janet's 'Art Deco watches' product

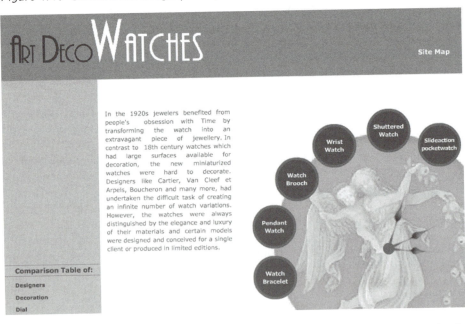

In the 1920s jewelers benefited from people's obsession with Time by transforming the watch into an extravagant piece of jewellery. In contrast to 18th century watches which had large surfaces available for decoration, the new miniaturized watches were hard to decorate. Designers like Cartier, Van Cleef et Arpels, Boucheron and many more, had undertaken the difficult task of creating an infinite number of watch variations. However, the watches were always distinguished by the elegance and luxury of their materials and certain models were designed and conceived for a single client or produced in limited editions.

*Figure 4.50* Home page from Christina, Rachel and Mohamed's 'Art Deco watches' product

The 'watches' table in this case is translated metaphorically as a clock dial, with the types of watches forming the digits and functioning as navigation buttons. The translation is metaphorical because a real-world object, namely a clock face, is used to translate more abstract and general categories (types of watches).

## The network

We have already given some examples of the implicit translation of network relations into text and by juxtaposition (Figures 4.2 and 4.6), as well as some examples of covert translations into navigation by underlined wordings – a kind of navigation buttons (Figure 4.4). Overt translations of semantic networks seem to appear only in specialized new media products such as the Visual Thesaurus, where they are used to graphically represent the relationships of words to each other (see Figure 4.51).

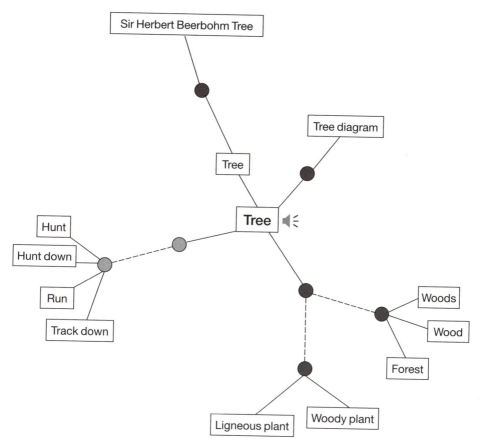

*Figure 4.51* Page from the Visual Thesaurus (www.visualthesaurus.com)

Translating networks into navigation devices commonly takes the form of a horizontal navigation bar, usually at the top but sometimes also at the bottom of a screen. An example is shown in Figure 4.52.

The navigation buttons are simply a list of topics associated with one another in some way. In this particular case (people, services, publications, events), the association seems to be something like: *people – perform – services, people – produce – publications, people – organize – events*. But the connection between the topics can be looser than this. The Yahoo! 'Services' section (see Figure 4.53), for example, consists of navigation buttons whose topics are related only insofar as they all belong to the semantic field of 'services'.

As for other types of second translation, we have not come across translations of networks into interfaces – whether as arrangements of headings, as other non-linear models or as image processes. Neither have we seen metaphorical translations of networks, although it would not be difficult to think of semantic networks being translated as some kind of a physical network, such as a network of different kinds of roads representing different semantic relations and towns and cities representing semantic nodes. One of the advantages of a systematic approach such as ours is that it brings gaps to light – design solutions that are evidently possible, but have apparently been overlooked, perhaps because, in the absence of systematic exploration, most design ideas tend to be variations of ideas that have already been explored before.

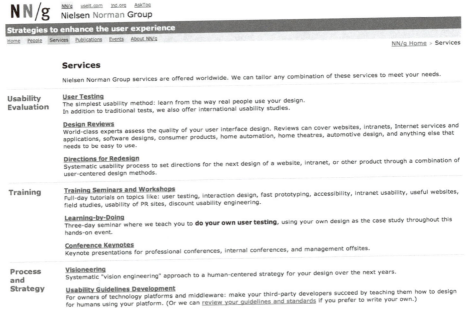

*Figure 4.52* Page from Jakob Nielsen's website (www.useit.com)

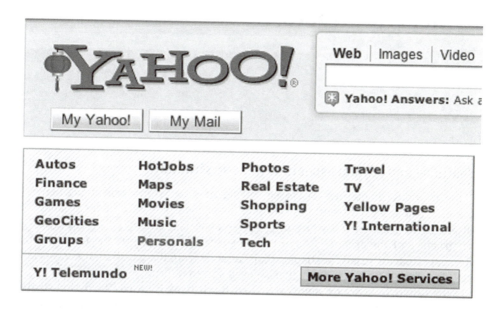

*Figure 4.53* Page from Yahoo! website (www.yahoo.com)

# 5 Generic structure

## Ideational and textual aspects of generic structure

In the previous chapter we discussed individual screens and transitions between screens. But the second translations of non-linear models in new media products do not appear in isolation. They are always interconnected, creating different layers in the structure of the products. As already discussed in Chapter 1, the forms of this interconnectedness result, or should result, directly from the selection of appropriate design strategies. So it is to these that we need now to return.

In the systemic theory of language on which this book is based, the design strategies of linguistic texts are called genres (cf. e.g. Martin 1992; van Leeuwen 2005). Genres are types of texts that differ in terms of the goals they are designed to achieve. The goals determine the genres' semantic characteristics, and are realized progressively as the text unfolds, giving different genres distinct staging structures. To take a simple example, an advertisement that uses a 'problem–solution' strategy usually consists of at least three stages, a problem (for instance headache), a solution (the advertised medicine) and a recommendation to buy the advertised product. Each stage has its own goal, e.g. establishing that there is a problem (suffering from headache), suggesting the solution (suggesting that the product is the answer), etc. and taken together, in their particular order, the stages realize the overall strategy through which the advertiser tries to achieve his/her aim.

From this point of view of the ideational meaning (see Chapter 1), genres are distinct text types with particular text structures. In our experience, this ideational aspect of new media design genres does not yet appear to be well established. The examples of correlations of strategies with different non-linear models that we presented in Chapter 1 are only tentative and only regard the simple non-linear models that are at the centre of the complex model that a strategy correlates with. Although we have not investigated the ideational aspect of genres systematically, it seems to us that only two combinations of simple non-linear models remotely approach the status of established, recurrent types: a tree with branches linked by network relations, and a star with trees sub-classifying the satellites. The tree-network complex non-linear model seems to be more firmly established than the star-trees model.

As for the progressive unfolding of the translation of the tree-network model into a new media product, screen content navigated by the top-left corner covert tree and by implicitly translated network links in text is the most well established pattern. This is no doubt because it had already been established in print, in the form of the two kinds of book navigation, the chapter of contents and the index. We have however noted the disadvantages of an excessive and unmodified adoption of this form of navigation for new media design. The only second translation of the star-trees complex model that approaches any degree of being established is by a heading above a horizontal navigation bar at the top of the page at the first layer of structure, followed by covert translations in navigation of the trees at the second layer. Even the use of this pattern is however quite unsystematic, as we will see in our analysis and redesign of an existing website in Chapter 6.

So far, we have been talking about the cognitive, or *ideational* (Halliday 1994) meaning, or aspect of genres. However, the stages of generic structures can also be seen as having a *textual* aspect. From the point of view of the ideational meaning, different genres are unlike one another, having distinct semantic characteristics and staging structures. In terms of their textual aspect, however, their structures are very much the same. We already touched on the textual meaning or function briefly in Chapter 1. Oversimplifying somewhat, one might say that, whereas the ideational aspect of genre has to do with *what* the components of the sequence of stages are, the textual aspect has to do with *how* the sequencing is done. It is about the packaging, or articulation, of the ideational content. This involves a hierarchy by means of which the ideational content is *outlined* on a page at one layer of a product's structure, then *condensed* in the labels of the navigation buttons on the same page, and finally *expanded* on the pages of the next layer of structure. This more or less regular, iterative or periodic articulation of content has been called a hierarchy of periodicity by Halliday (in Thibault 1987) and Martin (1992). One such cycle of the periodic structure is represented in Figure 5.1.

As Figure 5.1 shows, an outline at one layer follows an expansion of the outline and navigation buttons at the preceding layer. The home page is an exception since it is the first page and does not expand any outline or navigation buttons. At the same time, the main part of its content and the outline of the next layer may be fused. As an example, consider our complex non-linear model of the 'polyphonic music' text (Figure 3.1), which had a tree at the first level of structure and a star with two satellites at the second. In translating this model, the content of the tree's root (*singing in parts*) would be mapped onto the title and the main part of the content of the home page. The content of the two subordinate nodes (*parallel organum* and *free organum*) would be outlined at the bottom of the page or fused with the other text on the page and condensed in the navigation buttons, forming the first layer of navigation. The condensed content of the free organum subordinate, which is at the same time the nucleus of the second-level star, would then be expanded into the title and the main part of the page at the second layer of the product structure. One generic stage thus corresponds to a node at one level of the non-linear structure, together with the line leading to a node at the next-higher level. The line represents the relationship that obtains between the nodes – a tree, star, network, etc. – which is translated by the layout and position on the page of the navigation buttons. The correspondence for the above example is represented in Figure 5.2.

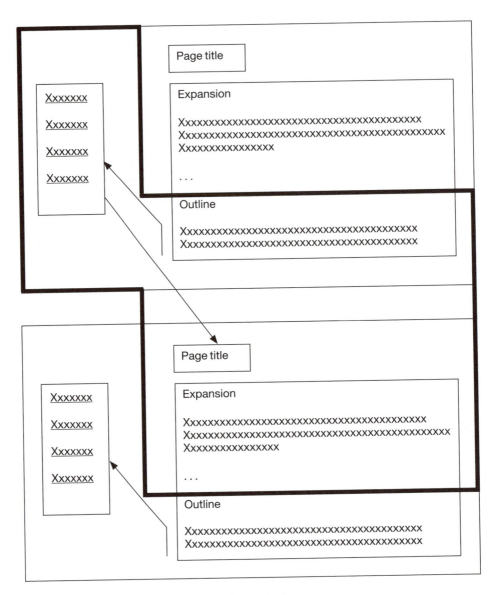

*Figure 5.1*    Generic stage in new media products

## Variations of the basic pattern

The pattern we have just described can be varied in a number of ways. The outline of the content of the next-lower layer of structure, for instance, is optional. However, in that case what follows should be inferable from the rest of the page. If there is not much content in the nodes of a non-linear model, a whole page or even a whole layer

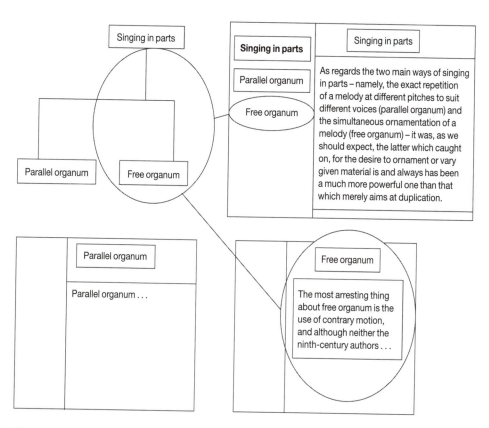

*Figure 5.2* Correspondences between a generic stage in a non-linear model and a layer of a new media product

of a product structure can be left out in the translation. This is what happened in one of the student products we already discussed (see Figure 4.36). Here the satellites of the main star were not outlined on the home page, but directly represented in condensed form, as first-layer navigation buttons, and the content of these navigation buttons was not expanded on the pages of the second-layer structure either. Instead there was a jump directly to the second-layer navigation buttons, and it was only the condensed content of these buttons that was expanded on the pages of the third layer of the site's structure. Only the specific types of guns (arquebus, musket, etc.) received a page of their own, for example. More generally, there did not seem to be a need for a whole second layer of structure in translations of the 'guns' text, since the navigation paths from the home page to the third layer of structure, via the two layers of navigation buttons, seemed self-explanatory. It was obviously not by chance that the more general categories that form the satellites of the *guns* nucleus did not occur in the original text. There, too, it was assumed that readers would be able to infer them.

There is, however, a need for at least some information to set the context for the whole site or to clarify its purpose, whether on the home page or in some other kind of introduction. The short piece of text on the home page shown in Figure 4.36 suggests that the primary concern of the site relates to the effects of the invention of guns, as reflected in the navigation buttons titled *effects on civilization* and *effects on warfare*. This, however, does not predict the other three buttons: *types*, *equipments* and *innovators*. The text should therefore have been expanded to include a reference to, or an outline of, these other semantic fields as well.

The introduction to another product based on the 'guns' text, represented in Figures 4.13 and 4.14, was somewhat more substantial, promising to answer questions about the origins of guns. This corresponds much better to the topics the students included in their non-linear model and product: *gun invention, gun trouble, types of guns, gun power* and *gun battle* (see Figure 4.12). Only *gun battle* led to content about the consequences of guns and was therefore not predicted by the introduction. Yet another student project (shown in Figure 4.7) did not have any text at all on the home page, nor any form of introduction to specify its purpose. The goal of the site therefore remained rather unclear and the design less than optimal.

Another way of leaving out a layer of structure is to use what otherwise would be the title of a page on which content is expanded as a non-clickable heading for navigation buttons that translate subordinate nodes. Figure 5.3 is an example. On this

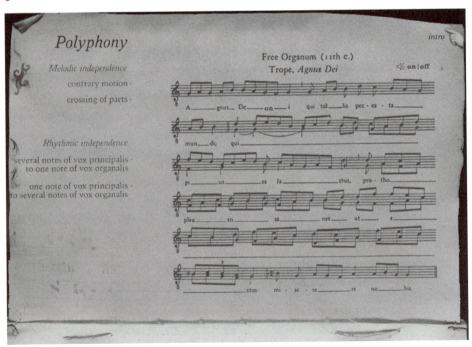

*Figure 5.3*  Page from the 'polyphonic music' product of Harry, Froukje and Emily

page, *melodic independence* and *rhythmic independence* are used as non-clickable headings while *contrary motion* and *crossing of parts*, and *several notes of vox principalis to one note of vox organalis* and *one note of vox principalis to several notes of vox organalis*, translate the subordinate nodes of the non-linear models (cf. the model in Figure 3.1).

In Figure 5.4, a first-layer navigation button of a product whose home page we presented in Figure 4.31 is expanded into a page title and a fairly short text that captures the essence of the content of the satellite/superordinate − 'The gun had two profound consequences for the shaping of modern civilization.' The two kinds of consequences ('It reduced the significance of the castle and the city as containers of military power' and 'It helped to shift battles away from castles and cities') outline the third layer of structure. They are, however, also clickable, and so at the same time form the second layer of navigation. Clicking on them makes more text and images appear in the window on the left side of the screen, which thus represents the third layer of structure. This is an interesting solution, whose use of the window and the fusion of the outline with navigation buttons is very economical, although we would have preferred to see the left and right sides of the screen reversed since the text and the clickable outline belong to the second layer of the product's structure, and so should logically be the Given, whereas the window belongs to the third layer, which should be the New.

Another interesting solution to the realization of the hierarchy of periodicity is the use of images rather than language, as, e.g., in Figure 5.5.

The product begins with a Flash introduction outlining the site's main topics. It takes the form of a succession of questions such as 'What was one of the momentous changes in history?', 'What was Europe's involvement?', 'Who was Gustavus Adolphus?', 'Do you ever think about war?', 'How did the military change?' and 'Is there such a thing as a two-man gun?'. The screen then changes into a large question mark followed by the overt translation of the star (shown in Figure 5.5), which is the central element in the non-linear model on which the product is based (shown in Figure 5.6).

The second translation is based on the similarity of the star model to a revolver cylinder, which is not a true metaphor but only a similarity of physical form, a kind of visual rhyme. The chambers representing the satellites function as navigation buttons and clicking on any one of them makes the overt star recede into the background, so turning it into a navigation menu. Simultaneously, a classificational image process (Kress and van Leeuwen 2007) appears in the foreground, expanding the content of the related navigation button, as shown in Figure 5.7.

The navigation buttons in the overt star condense the content outlined in the site's introduction. The image process title, which repeats the title of the related navigation button, is analogous to the title of the page which, in a more traditional product, would expand the content condensed in the navigation button. The images below the title are rollover navigation buttons. On rolling over, they reveal the name of the type of gun or whatever other content they represent, as well as a short exhortation to

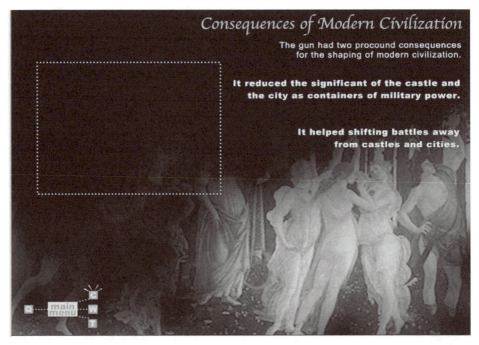

*Figure 5.4* Screen from 'guns' product by Gunther, Terry and Jim

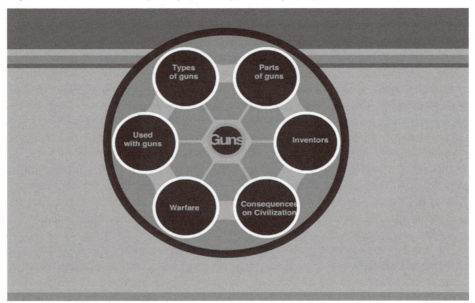

*Figure 5.5* 'Revolver drum' screen from the 'guns' product of Jill, Anne and Veronica

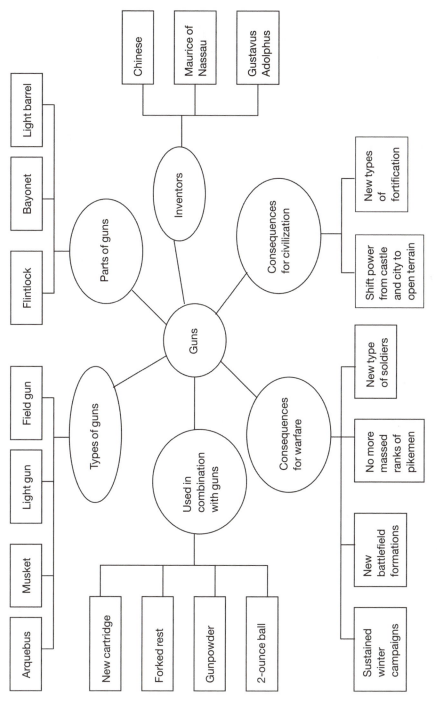

*Figure 5.6* Jill, Anne and Veronica's non-linear model of the 'guns' text

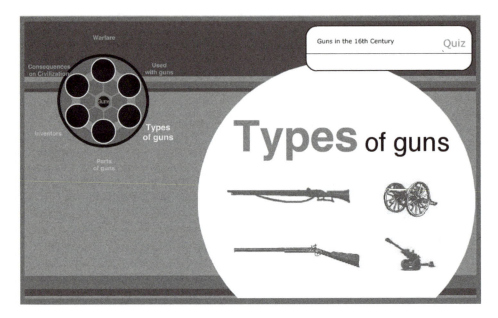

*Figure 5.7* '16th century guns' screen from Jill, Anne and Veronica's 'guns' product

click for more information. They are thus analogous to the covert tree navigation menus typically found in the top-left corner of traditional websites. After clicking on a navigation button, a short text appears next to the image process, expanding the content condensed in the navigation button (see Figure 5.8).

The classificational image process used here is thus analogous to the second layer of structure of more traditional products, while the introduction and the overt star navigation menu are analogous to the first layer and the text to the third layer.

## Generic structure in translations of the 'polyphonic music' text

In this section we look at some of the second translations of the 'polyphonic music' text from the point of view of generic structure. The students whose home page is shown in Figure 5.9 faithfully followed the basic generic structure outlined above.

The home page sets the context for the content of the whole product, making clear that the product is about changes in the history of music that took place in the eleventh century. It also outlines what the next layer of structure will be about, namely parallel and free organa. This outline is condensed in the first layer of navigation buttons (*Parallel organum* and *Free organum*). Clicking on *Parallel organum* takes the user to a page with an explanation of what parallel organum is as well as an illustration by means of a note stave and a sound sample (see Figure 5.10).

Clicking on *Free organum* leads to a page with a brief explanation of free organum and an illustration of the concept by a note staff and a sound sample. There is also an

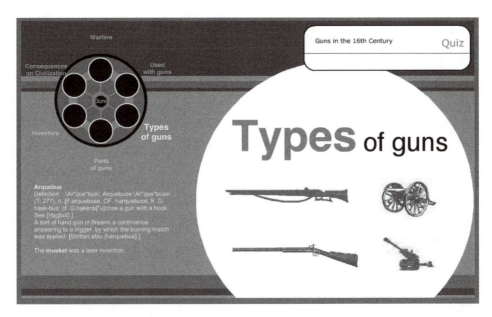

*Figure 5.8* '16th century guns' screen with explanation of arquebus, from the 'guns' product of Jill, Anne and Veronica

outline of the next layer of the structure which deals with free organum's two attributes of *Melodic independence* and *Rhythmic independence* and which is condensed in the two navigation buttons at the bottom of the page. Finally, there is a network link to the theorists of the era, leading to a page discussing Guido d'Arezzo's and John Cotton's contributions to the history of music (see Figure 5.11).

The *Melodic independence* and *Rhythmic independence* buttons lead to pages with information about these important characteristics of free organum. When the buttons are clicked, the pages appear, together with the navigation buttons that lead to the next-lower layer of structure. Clicking on the *Rhythmic independence* button thus leads to the page represented in Figure 5.12.

There is a very short introduction to rhythmic independence ('Rhythmic independence is the second of two essential characteristics of free organum (or polyphony)'), followed by an outline of the fourth layer of structure ('To make a piece of music rhythmically independent, the composer has to choose one of two options'). The outline is condensed in the navigation buttons (*Early practice* and *Later practice*). Then there is a brief discussion of the difficulties with synchronization of the different voices, with a link that leads to a page where the three methods of synchronization proposed in the text are briefly mentioned and illustrated as navigation buttons (see Figure 5.13).

The navigation buttons lead to the next-lower layer of structure where the methods of synchronization are each discussed in more detail (see Figure 5.14 for the page that deals with the score method).

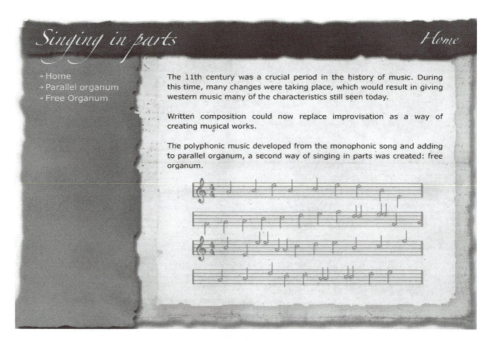

Figure 5.9 Home page of the 'polyphonic music' product of Laura, Pilar and Bessie

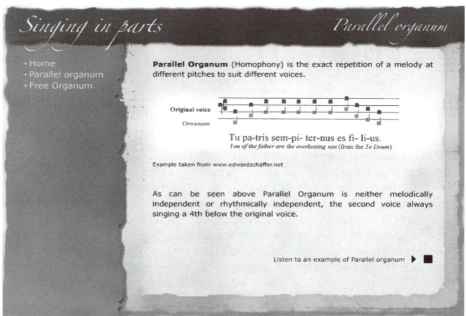

Figure 5.10 'Parallel organum' page from the 'polyphonic music' product of Laura, Pilar and Bessie

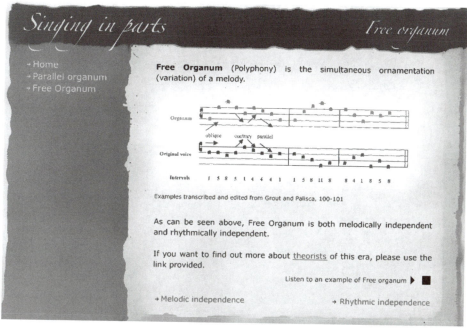

→ Home
→ Parallel organum
→ Free Organum

**Free Organum** (Polyphony) is the simultaneous ornamentation (variation) of a melody.

Examples transcribed and edited from Grout and Palisca, 100-101

As can be seen above, Free Organum is both melodically independent and rhythmically independent.

If you want to find out more about theorists of this era, please use the link provided.

Listen to an example of Free organum ▶ ▮

→ Melodic independence                    → Rhythmic independence

*Figure 5.11* 'Free organum' page from the 'polyphonic music' product of Laura, Pilar and Bessie

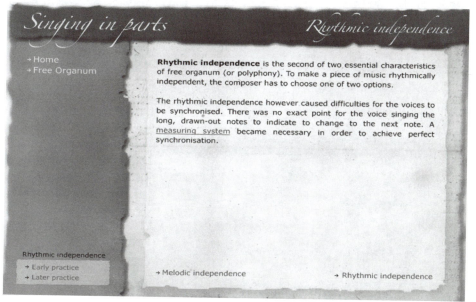

→ Home
→ Free Organum

**Rhythmic independence** is the second of two essential characteristics of free organum (or polyphony). To make a piece of music rhythmically independent, the composer has to choose one of two options.

The rhythmic independence however caused difficulties for the voices to be synchronised. There was no exact point for the voice singing the long, drawn-out notes to indicate to change to the next note. A measuring system became necessary in order to achieve perfect synchronisation.

Rhythmic independence
→ Early practice
→ Later practice

→ Melodic independence                    → Rhythmic independence

*Figure 5.12* 'Rhythmic independence' page from the 'polyphonic music' product of Laura, Pilar and Bessie

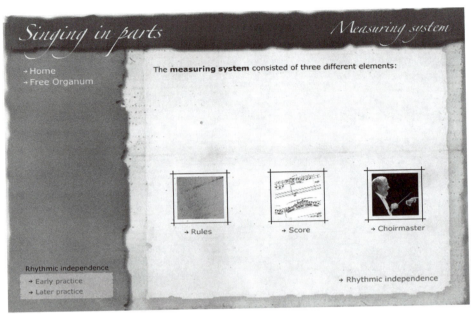

*Figure 5.13* 'Measuring system' page from the 'polyphonic music' product of Laura, Pilar and Bessie

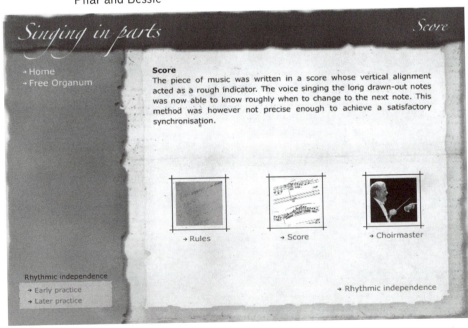

*Figure 5.14* 'Score' page from the 'polyphonic music' product of Laura, Pilar and Bessie

We find this second translation of the 'polyphonic music' text quite successful. Its periodic structure usefully and explicitly parcels and articulates the rather complex content of the product and the product is therefore much easier to understand than the original text, and of course also much more interesting because of the illustrations and sound samples.

Another student translation of the 'polyphonic music' text structures the hierarchy of periodicity less carefully. It has an introduction and a main part in which the various characteristics of polyphony are discussed and exemplified. The introduction defines the two kinds of 'singing in parts', with the definitions appearing one at a time, beginning with homophony. Homophony is defined as 'Parallel organum, the exact repetition of a melody at different pitches to suit different voices' and polyphony as 'Free organum, the simultaneous ornamentation of a melody' (see Figure 5.15). Besides these definitions, however, no other information is provided, and it is therefore difficult to identify the purpose of the product.

Clicking on *enter* takes the user to the main part of the site which is represented in Figure 5.16.

The page consists of a navigation menu on the left and, on the right, a window that fills up with content when the navigation buttons are clicked. The window is linked to the *Polyphony* button and displays a stave, accompanied by a sound sample. There is no discussion of polyphony at this first layer of structure. *Melodic independence* and *Rhythmic independence* are just non-clickable headings that do not lead to any content. Except for the headings then, the second layer of structure is left out. The subordinate buttons of *contrary motion, crossing of parts*, etc. each lead to a demonstration of the concepts by means of animated notes, below which related excerpts from the original 'music' text are displayed in a smaller window (see Figure 5.17).

The text that appears after clicking on *contrary motion* begins with 'The most arresting thing about free organum is the use of contrary motion'. Users who are accustomed to non-linear thinking or who are experts on polyphonic music may be able to infer from this short introduction that contrary motion is a kind of melodic independence; that melodic independence, in turn, is an attribute of polyphony; and that polyphony is another word for free organum. But we think that most users would find this part of the product's content difficult to understand. The difficulty increases as one reaches the attempt to explain the 'crossing of parts'. Clicking on the navigation button leads again to an animated demonstration of the concept and an explanatory text underneath. But the text focuses on the crossing of parts and does not place this concept in the wider context of melodic independence and polyphony. The same is true of the content that appears after clicking on the two subordinates of *Rhythmic independence*.

What is missing here are the semantic *relations* between the concepts of the non-linear model – the links that would scaffold and make explicit the meaning of the new media content by means of the periodic structuring we explain and exemplify in this chapter.

*Figure 5.15* Title page of the 'polyphonic music' product of Harry, Froukje and Emily

*Figure 5.16* Intro page from the 'polyphonic music' product of Harry, Froukje and Emily

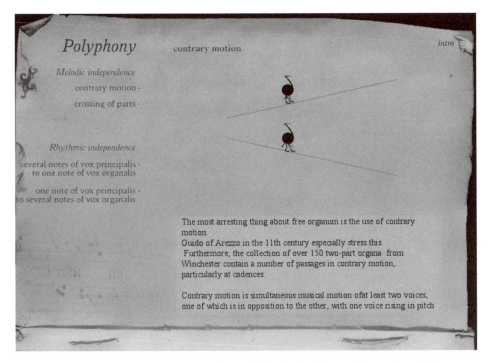

*Figure 5.17* 'Contrary motion' page from the 'polyphonic music' product of Harry, Froukje and Emily

## Generic structure in translations of the 'Art Deco watches' text

We will now compare some student translations of the 'Art Deco watches' text from the point of view of their generic structure. The first one uses a fair amount of text and has a clear generic structure. Its home page is represented in Figure 5.18.

After a short introduction, the page outlines the purpose of the product: 'This website is a small showcase of the watches and the timepieces of that period. It features jewellery designers and watchmakers who helped to set standards for stylish, lavish timepieces.' The first-layer navigation menu is a revolving ring of watch images and labels at the top of the page. Clicking leads to a page with a larger image of the relevant watch, accompanied by a text describing it in terms of attributes from the table on which this product is based. Each page translates one of the rows from the table, with the independent variable, i.e. the watch type, translated as a labelled image, and the dependent variables translated implicitly, as textual descriptions (see Figure 5.19).

In terms of generic structure, the image–text combination expands the related navigation button. There is no outline of the third layer of structure in the text, but since this second layer is about a watch made by a particular manufacturer (Boucheron), users can probably infer that the navigation buttons in the bottom-left corner

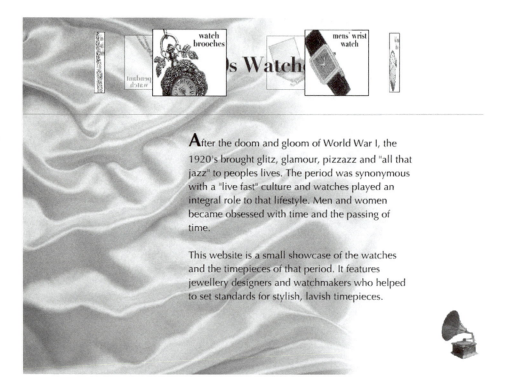

*Figure 5.18* Home page of the 'Art Deco watches' product of Sarah, David and Betsy

are expanded by pages with image–text combinations describing ladies' watch brooches made by other manufacturers, namely Cartier and Marchak. Including the Boucheron button in this second-layer navigation menu is perhaps confusing and the button might have been replaced by a superordinate such as *Other watch brooches*, in a larger bold type.

Our second example makes much greater use of images. We have already discussed it from the point of view of the second translation of its non-linear model, which is a table (see Figure 4.49), and we will now discuss the generic structure of the product as a whole. As we have seen (Figures 4.19 and 4.20), the introduction to this product consists of an illustrated implicit translation of a Given–New structure dealing with the social and technological context of the 1920s and its effects on watch production. While the introduction unfolds, different watch types drawn in red rise from the wrists, chests, etc. of the people represented in the images, forming the first-layer navigation menu in the top-right corner of the screen (see Figure 5.20).

The images of the watch types in the navigation buttons are predicted by the introduction and can, to some extent, be said to condense it. Clicking on any one of them expands it rather literally into a window with a larger, naturalistic image and drawings of the parts the watch consists of (see Figure 5.21).

Fancy brooch watches in the twenties were very extravagent. The Boucheron brooch in a bud-shape with leaves, consists of a watch in the shape of a pansy hanging from it. Both are set with diamonds, garnets and amethysts. Coloured stones and diamonds were very common for brooch watches in a figurative form. The dial was often hidden or miniscule.

*Figure 5.19* 'Ladies' watch brooch' page from Sarah, David and Betsy's 'Art Deco watches' product

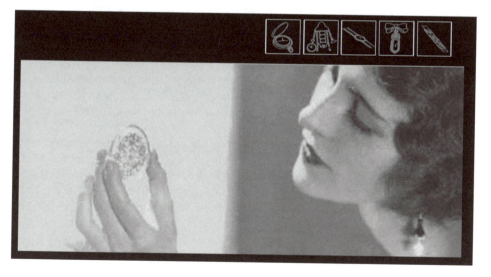

*Figure 5.20* Screen from the introduction of Brogan, Philip and Janet's 'Art Deco watches' product

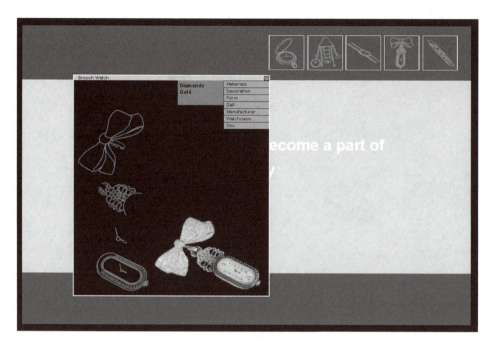

*Figure 5.21* 'Brooch watch' page from the 'Art Deco watches' product of Brogan,
        Philip and Janet

Together with the label for the type of watch in the top-left corner of the image
frame, the image is analogous to a page with a title and a textual expansion at the
second layer of structure. There is a navigation menu in the top-right corner of the
image process, with buttons that represent the attribute types from the watch table
(e.g. *materials, decoration*). Rolling over the buttons leads to the appearance of
the values of these dependent variables that are specific to the type of watch displayed
(e.g. *diamonds, gold*). Rolling over these buttons leads to labels appearing on the
relevant parts of the watches in the image process.

The menu of the attribute types belongs to the second layer of the product's structure and the more detailed menu buttons and labels associated with the watch parts to
the third layer. The second layer of structure consists entirely of an image (as do the
first-layer navigation buttons), so there is no outline of the third layer of structure to
be condensed in the second layer of navigation and expanded in the third layer of
structure. There is, however, a general-to-specific relationship between the parts of
the watch and the attribute types in the navigation menu (the attribute-type labels
give the user an idea of what the image parts are), and between the attribute types
and their specific values in the more detailed menu items and labels on the watch
parts. The two cycles of general-to-specific content can be considered as analogous to
an outline–condensation–expansion cycle in more traditionally designed websites.

We will end by analysing one of the metaphorical translations of the 'watches' table for its generic structure. We have already encountered this product in Figure 4.33. It has a short animated introduction, where the location and the characters of the narrative scenario make their first appearance. The location is a watch shop and the characters are the shop owner, Mr Fast, and three well-off women and two men, who pass by the shop with thought bubbles next to their heads. The characters' thoughts reflect the influence of the social and technological context of the 1920s on the quality, design and price of watches as well as on men's and women's obsession with time. The women's thoughts are: 'Mr Fast always knows what will flatter me', 'I know I have spent too much already but James won't mind' and 'I do like those new bracelet watches. They are so daring!'. The men's thoughts are: 'Those new mechanisms are remarkable' and 'I am in a hurry, I hope he has what I want'.

After the introduction, the scene changes to the inside of the watch shop with the shop owner in the centre, behind his desk, saying, through a speech bubble: 'Good day, time travellers. I am Mr Fast, purveyor of fine watches. Please come and explore my shop to find out more about the evolution of watch design!' The scene is represented in Figure 4.33 and the various navigation hotspots that are part of it have already been discussed. Mr Fast's welcome functions as an introduction to a metaphorical translation of the complex non-linear model (which we reproduced in Figure 3.9), and is analogous to introductions on the home pages of more traditional new media products. The metaphorical translation of the *manufacturers* satellite is the *Manufacturers* heading on the *Live Fast Collection* information board. The *types of watches* satellite is not translated but left as the implicit superordinate of the watch types displayed in the case in the background of the shop. The *mechanisms* satellite is translated by an image of the uncovered mechanism of the clock standing on the billiard table. Finally, the *materials* satellite is translated as the billiard balls made up of various kinds of stones. In a more traditional design, the satellites would instead form a first-layer navigation bar at the top of the home page.

Clicking on the hotspots leads to further speech bubbles from Mr Fast. Clicking on *Manufacturers* results in a speech bubble explaining the influence of the 1920s obsession with time on the success of both jewellers' and mass production watches: 'The men and women of the 1920s were obsessed with the passing of time. Jewelers understood the capital they could make out of this useful object . . .' Clicking on the types-of-watches display brings up a speech bubble with a general introduction to ladies' and men's watch design: 'An inventive richness went into the design not only of ladies' watches, but also of men's.' Clicking on the watch mechanism results in a speech bubble describing the mechanical innovations that led to the miniaturization of watch mechanisms: 'In the early 1800s the mechanisms were large and heavy. Mechanical advances and innovations by the watch making industries – for example the use of platinum movements – meant that they became smaller and lighter.' Finally, clicking on the billiard balls leads to a speech bubble describing watchmaking materials: 'In the 18th century, the watch, with its chatelaine and hanging ornaments, had offered large surfaces for decoration with enamel, diamonds and gemstones. Later, the dials were reduced to microscopic dimensions.' Simultaneously with the speech bubbles, illustrations of the concepts mentioned (e.g. of the different kinds of materials or mechanisms) appear in the *Information* section in the bottom-left corner of the screen. The speech bubbles, combined with the relevant illustrations, are analogous to the content of the pages in the second layer of structure of a more traditional new media product. They expand, or elaborate on, the content that is condensed in the hotspots.

The watchmakers' names on the information board are analogous to the navigation buttons on a second-layer page about manufacturers in general. Clicking on them leads to another set of the shop owner's speech bubbles, each of them providing information about specific manufacturers: 'One of the most innovative clockmakers of his time, Jean-Simon Bourdier became a maitre horologer in Paris in 1787 . . . . The prestigious Swiss watch manufacturer Van Cleef et Arpel was founded in 1906 and is one of the world's leading manufacturers and retailers of jewelry and watches . . . . Cartier was founded in 1847 by Louis-Francois Cartier, son of a Parisian powder horn maker. Cartier's jewelry was characterized by a light, airy touch in contrast to the overly formal and overwrought ornaments of the period', etc. Simultaneously with this information, illustrations of watches made by the manufacturers and some additional information appear in the *Information* section. The information in the speech bubbles, together with the illustrations and additional information, expands the hotspots and is analogous to pages at the third layer of structure of more traditional products.

Two network links (*ladies'* and *men's*) in a speech bubble containing the general introduction to types of watches lead to further speech bubbles with more specific information about the different watch types. The *ladies'* link leads to: 'Ladies' watch designs included the bracelet watch, the pendant or chatelaine watch, and the brooch watch. The dial was often hidden . . . . Ladies watches were also sometimes hidden in cigarette boxes and lighters, powder compacts and lipstick cases . . . . Ladies watch bracelets, invented towards the end of the 18th century, became popular again at the beginning of the 20th century, when fashion no longer required long sleeves . . . . The pendant or chatelaine watch was popular between 1925 and 1930. They were one of the most popular designs of Van Cleef et Arpel.' The *men's* link leads to: 'The pocket or fob watch was the original type of watch used by men . . . . The fob watch evolved into a shuttered watch, disguised in a watch case in the form of a lighter . . . . The wristwatch gradually took preference over the pocket watch because of its practicality.' As these speech bubbles appear, images of the various watch types are displayed in the *Information* section of the interface. These more detailed descriptions and illustrations of the different types of watches expand the general introduction to the watch types and are analogous to the third layer of structure in more traditional products.

Parts of the complex non-linear model that motivates this product are translated by another portion of the narrative scenario. Clicking on the icons of the different characters in the bottom-left corner of the screen leads to their interaction with the shop owner who provides information about other kinds of watches. For example, clicking on the gentleman with the bowler hat leads to his animated figure entering the shop and saying: 'I would like to replace my fob watch with something smaller to go racing; it's too big and cumbersome.' To which the shop owner answers: 'Certainly Sir. Perhaps you would like to try one of these wristwatches by Cartier?' Simultaneously with his answer, information about wristwatches appears in the *Information* section, accompanied by an image of a wristwatch. A little later, the scene grows dark and only Cartier's name is highlighted on the information board, together with an image of a fob watch in the watch display on the wall and with one of the billiard balls. The question and answer, together with the general information about wristwatches in the *Information* section, are analogous to a page at the second layer of structure, and the highlighted hotspots are equivalent to second-layer navigation buttons.

One would expect the hotspots to lead to information about Cartier wristwatches and to fob watches and the materials that they or wristwatches are made of. Unfortunately, this expectation is fulfilled only in relation to the Cartier hotspot. As already mentioned, clicking on the fob watch leads to the shop owner's speech bubble with general information about all the different types of watches and clicking on the billiard ball leads to the speech bubble with general information about materials used to make watches in that era. If all this information had been more specifically related to the fob or wristwatches, the hotspots would have led to what would have been an analogy of the third layer of structure in a more traditional translation and that would have expanded the content of the hotspots along the lines we have recommended in this chapter.

We found this translation quite successful because it makes creative use of metaphor and at the same time remains quite rigorously motivated by the non-linear model that underlies it. It is true that the translation does not include the meaning of comparison, as we pointed out in Chapter 3, but this is more a matter of the first translation. Given that the star model was chosen, it is difficult not to appreciate the combination of creative design and analytical rigour that characterized this group's translation.

# 6 Case studies

Most of our examples so far were student exercises intended to put our method into practice. In this final chapter we present two case studies of existing internet sites (both accessed in September 2006) – ShopNike.com and the website of the Calvary Presbyterian Church in San Francisco. The two sites differ in terms of their purposes, or strategies, and consequently also in terms of their non-linear structure. ShopNike.com is the online store of the Nike.com site and aims at presenting an assortment of sporting goods for online selection and purchase. The Calvary Presbyterian Church website presents information about the church to make it known in cyberspace and probably also to attract new members.

We will start by extracting complex non-linear models from the two websites, based on their navigation structure and most obvious content structure. These will be presented in the usual diagrammatic form. We will then analyse a representative sample of the content of the two websites for its semantic structure, and design new non-linear models which more faithfully represent that structure. Following our second translation rules, we will finally translate these non-linear models into re-designed websites, which, we would argue, are better suited both to the non-linear semantics of their content and to the purposes, or strategies, of the sites.

## ShopNike.com

ShopNike.com is a section of the much larger Nike.com site. But it is self-sufficient, and the place where customers go shopping for various kinds of Nike products. We will first describe the site. As it is rather vast, we will restrict ourselves to a single path through it, focusing on different kinds of men's basketball shoes.

On arrival at ShopNike.com, users are presented with a home page and a navigation scheme (Figure 6.1). The home page has the headline 'More Air, More World' above a large image of a running shoe with a clickable caption: 'Air Max 360 ~ $160: *Men's Women's*'. At the bottom of the page, a navigation link says: 'See the Air Max Collection: *Men's Women's*.'

Clicking on *Women's* in the image caption leads directly to a page about the shoe, including another image of it, a description of its design and technology features, its price, choice of colours and similar details, and a link leading to the shopping cart (see Figure 6.2).

The left side of the home page features a large covert-tree navigation scheme, with headings and subheadings. As in many other websites, clicking on a heading reveals subheadings with subordinate content nodes. The main headings are *Men's*, *Women's*, *Kids'* and *Collections*. The subheadings under *Men's* are *All footwear*, *All apparel*, *All*

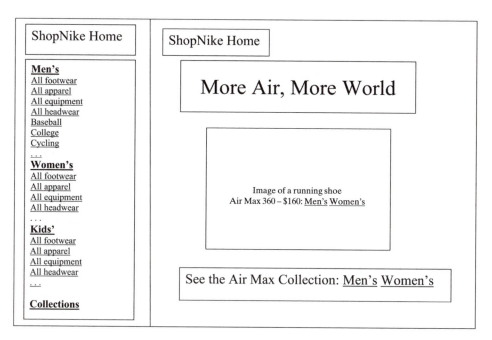

*Figure 6.1* ShopNike.com home page

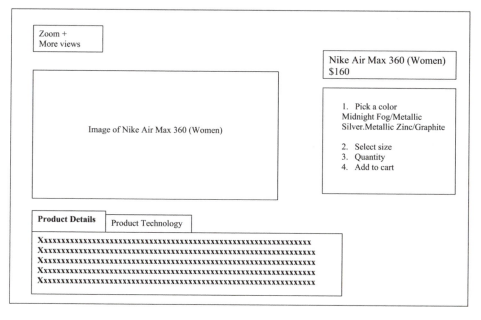

*Figure 6.2* Nike Air Max 360 (Women's) page

equipment, *All headwear, Baseball, Basketball, College, Cycling*, etc. Slightly differ-
ent subheadings can be found under *Women's* and *Kids'* headings. Following the
*Men's* path through the navigation, the subheadings under *All footwear* are *Air
Everywhere, Doernbecher Freestyle, Baseball, Basketball, College, Cycling*, etc. The
subheadings under *Basketball* are *Show all, Flight, Force, Uptempo, Signature* and
*Retro*.

Clicking on the *Men's* button in the covert navigation tree results in its highlighting
in orange and in another page replacing the home page, showing images of a sport
shoe (*Air Zoom Moire+ – Men's*), an iPodNano, a Nike+ iPod Sport Kit and a Nike+
Sport Armband, as well as of several kinds of 'Nike Favorites' and a customizable
running shoe. There is also a slogan, obviously related to the link-up between the
shoes and the iPod, which says 'Move in a New Direction. Revive your workout. Reen-
ergize yourself.' The images are clickable and lead directly to pages that are similar
to the page described above for *Nike Air Max 360 Women's*, where there is a detailed
description of the items and the option to place them in the shopping cart. The *Men's*
page is represented in Figure 6.3.

Clicking on the *All footwear* button highlights it in orange and changes the page to
one titled 'Free Your Game', with images of four versions of one shoe. The shoe is
presumably the Nike Free Trainer 7.0, which costs $75. This, however, is not easy to
determine at first, since the label *Nike Free Trainer 7.0* followed by the price tag
appears at the bottom of the page, fairly separate from the four images of the shoes.

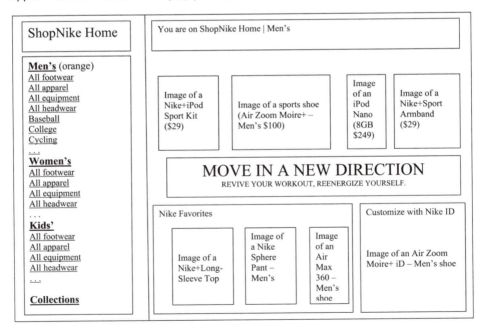

*Figure 6.3* ShopNike.com Men's home page

Both the images and the name of the shoe are clickable. When we clicked on the *Nike Free Trainer 7.0* link, we were not quite sure what kind of shoe the button would lead to, since we did not make the connection between it and the four image versions of the shoe. Clicking on one of the versions of the shoe in the images leads directly to that item on a similar page to the *Nike Airmax 360 Women's* one, with a similar blown-up image of the shoe, a detailed description and a link to the shopping cart. Clicking on the other versions leads to the same page with the shoes shown in different colours. The *All footwear* page is represented in Figure 6.4. Needless to say, and even more so than in the case of the *Men's* page, the content of this page does not make much sense because it is not related to the navigation button that leads to it.

Clicking on the *Basketball* button leads directly to the *Show all* page where all Nike basketball shoes are presented (see Figure 6.5).

The images of the basketball shoes are clickable and lead to pages with blown-up versions, detailed descriptions and a link to the shopping cart, similar to those we have already discussed. The *Basketball* navigation button is thus empty in the sense that there is no page at that level of structure.

Clicking on the *Force* button leads to a page with images of the basketball *Force* shoes (see Figure 6.6).

The images are again clickable and lead to pages with blown-up versions, accompanied by descriptions and links to the shopping cart. Figure 6.7 reproduces the page of *Nike Air Max 360 BBall*.

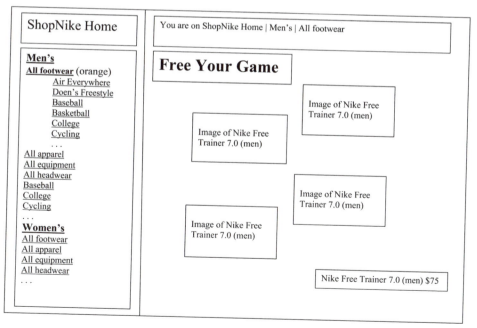

*Figure 6.4* ShopNike.com 'All footwear' page

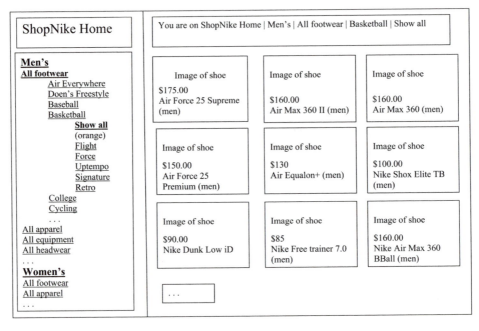

*Figure 6.5*  ShopNike.com 'Basketball/Show all' page

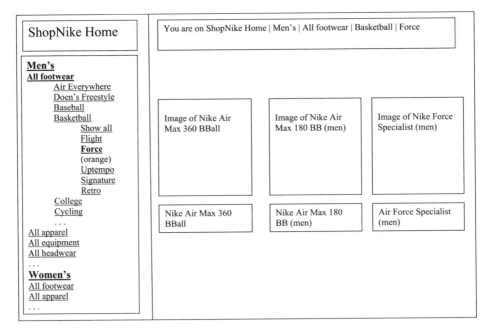

*Figure 6.6*  ShopNike.com 'Force shoes' page

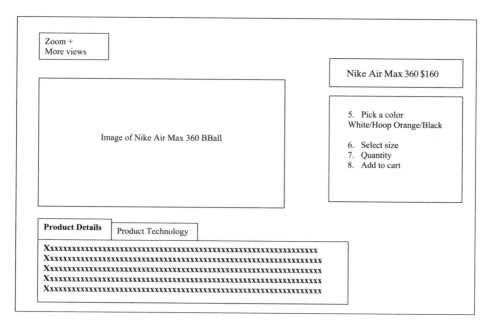

*Figure 6.7* ShopNike.com 'Nike Air Max 360 BBall' page

Based on the ShopNike.com navigation and content structure, we have extracted a non-linear model underlying the website structure by following our second translation rules (see Figure 6.8).

The model is a tree, with the first level (*men's, women's, kids', collections*) relating to the root (*ShopNike Home*) through a part–whole relationship, while the rest consists of classification relations. The final nodes in the tree all lead to content that is translated on the pages with detailed descriptions of the products and the shopping cart link (see Figures 6.2 and 6.7). According to our second translation rules, all these final pages are covert translations of rows in a table which is linked to the tree through network relations. The independent variables are the products themselves – *Nike Air Max 360 BBall, Nike Air Max 180 BB (men)*, etc. – and the dependent variables are their attributes. Only two of the attributes are translated in the main part of the page: colour and price. The other attributes are shown in the *Product Details* window.

For sports shoes, the text in the *Product Details* window consists of a description of four attributes – *upper, strap, sole* and *outsole*. An example description for *Nike Air Max 360 BBall* is:

Play on air in the Nike Air Max 360. The reloaded Force dominates the court with 360 degrees of Nike Max Air cushioning.

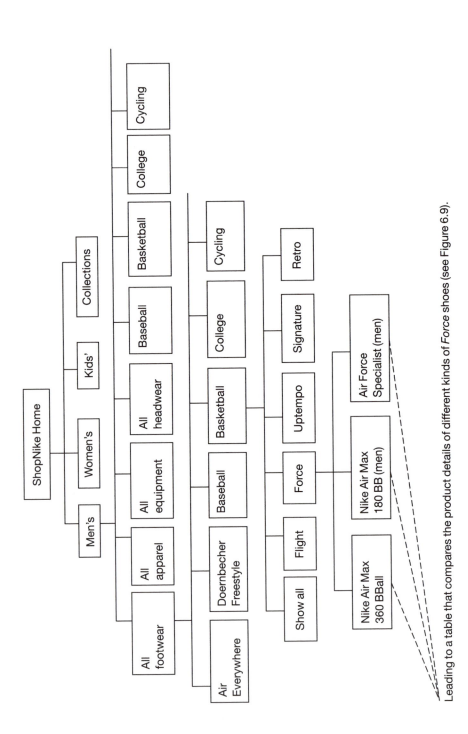

Leading to a table that compares the product details of different kinds of *Force* shoes (see Figure 6.9).

*Figure 6.8* The original non-linear structure of ShopNike.com

- Layered full-grain leather and premium synthetic upper delivers a supportive, protective fit for harnessing the power of the force player.
- Well-crafted, supportive strap improves protection and lockdown.
- Full-length engineered maximum Air-Sole unit provides cutting edge cushioning ride, and heel-to-heel toe transition.
- Solid and translucent rubber combination outsole with ribbed herringbone pattern promises max traction and foremost flexibility.

Each of the bullet-point entries consists of an outline of a feature of the shoe and its function. Each attribute in the table thus also includes both a feature and a function aspect. The table we extracted from the *Product Details* description of *Force* basketball shoes, as well as from their more prominently displayed attributes of colour and price, is shown in Figure 6.9.

Apart from the product features table with the 'design' and 'materials' features of the shoes, it also contains, rather less obviously, their technology features. These all have to do with the soles. As the table shows, *Nike Air Max 360 BBall* use a *Max Air* full-length, heel-to-toe sole unit. *Nike Air Max 180 BB (men)* have a *Max Air* heel unit and a forefoot *Zoom Air* unit. And *Air Force Specialist (men)* use *Air* units in their midsole.

More information about the technology features appears after clicking on the *Product Technology* button. Clicking on this button on the *Nike Air Max 360 BBall* page (see Figure 6.7) leads to the following description of *Max Air* technology:

Maximum impact cushioning. The brutal, repetitive, downward force of sport can wreak havoc on the body – and on performance. Max Air cushioning is specifically engineered to handle these impacts and provide protection. Max Air is big air designed to take a pounding. *See more*

Clicking on *see more* brings up a pop-up window with information about Nike Air, Max Air and Zoom Air technologies illustrated by images of shoes that incorporate these technologies. The window starts with Nike Air information and an image of a Nike Air shoe (see Figure 6.10).

Clicking on the *Get closer* link in the window leads to more information about Nike Air. Clicking on *Max Air* and *Zoom Air* brings up pop-up windows with information about Max Air and Zoom Air technologies. Clicking on *See Nike Air Products* leads to a ShopNike search engine page with more than 200 Nike Air products. Here is where the user's problems begin. *Air Everywhere* is the highest node in the overall navigation tree (see Figure 6.8), in which the *Air* designation appears, and it obviously has to do with *Air* technology. But why, if there are over 200 Nike Air products, does clicking on *Air Everywhere* lead only to four products – *Nike Air Max 360 BBall*, *Air Max 360 (men)*, *Nike Air Max 180 BB (men)* and *Air Max 180 (men)*? What is *Air Everywhere* anyway? What does it stand for and what is it opposed to? How is it related to *Air* in general, to *Nike Air* and the other kinds of *Air* technology

| | Upper feature/function | Strap feature/function | Sole feature/function | Outsole feature/function | Colour | Price |
|---|---|---|---|---|---|---|
| **Nike Air Max 360 BBall** | Layered full-grain leather and premium synthetic/delivers a supportive, protective fit for harnessing the power of the force player | Well-crafted, supportive strap/improves protection and lockdown | Full-length engineered maximum Air-Sole unit/provides cutting edge cushioning, ride, and heel-to-toe transition | Solid and translucent rubber combination outsole with ribbed herringbone pattern/ promises max traction and forefoot flexibility | White/Hoop Orange/Black | $160.00 |
| **Nike Air Max 180 BB (men)** | Premium synthetic and full-grain leather upper/provides incredible comfort and a protective fit | Removable strap/ offers enhanced ankle support | Double-lasted Phylon midsole, forefoot Zoom Air unit, and maximum heel Air-Sole unit/deliver incredible cushioning and responsiveness | Solid and translucent rubber outsole with ribbed herringbone pattern/offers maximum traction and forefoot flexibility | White/Black/ Varsity Royal | $120.00 |
| **Air Force Specialist (men)** | Upper combines leather and synthetics/for stability and comfort that's without peer | | Lightweight cushioned midsole featuring Air units/feels like walking on clouds | Solid rubber outsole/ grips the ground for maximum traction | White/White/ Black/Metallic Silver | $90.00 |

*Figure 6.9* Product features table for Nike basketball Force shoes

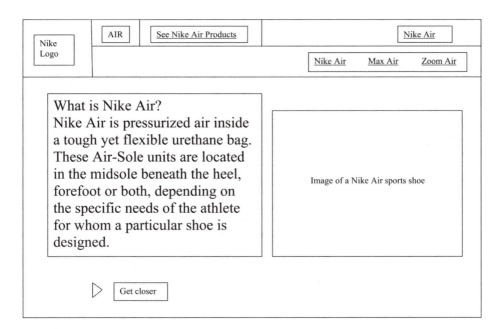

*Figure 6.10*  Nike Air pop-up window

(see the headings and navigation buttons in Figure 6.10)? Is *Air Max* in *Air Max 360 (men)* and other *Air Max* shoes the same as *Max Air* in *Max Air* technology? There are no answers to these questions on ShopNike.com. One could quite reasonably assume that *Air Everywhere* leads to shoes of which the entire sole is filled with *Air* units. The *Air Everywhere* button, however, leads to four *Air Max* shoes, and if one reads their description on the final pages, one realizes that *Air Everywhere* really means shoes that feature *Max Air* technology, and that this is what *Air Max* in their titles means. The numbers *360* and *180* indicate whether the *Max Air* unit extends along the whole sole or only a half of it.

Exploring the *Product Technology* pop-up further (see Figure 6.10) leads to more confusing information. Clicking on *Get closer* on the first page of the pop-up leads to another page where it is said that the *Nike Air* sole units are located in the midsole and beneath the heel or forefoot or both, but it does not say what the technology actually is. Clicking on *Max Air* on the first page leads to a page with information on *Visi Air*, which seems to be a different technology altogether. It is said to improve the effectiveness of the *Air* cushion by removing foam and replacing it with more durable *Air*. But it is nowhere said that *Nike Air* has foam – we thought it had air in it instead. The text goes on to say that *Visi Air* increases the volume of the *Air* unit and makes it visible through a window in the sidewall of the shoe. But the shoe that illustrates the text about *Nike Air* is the same as the shoe that illustrates this *Visi Air* text, and it has a window in the sidewall. The rest of the pages in the pop-up window just add to the overall confusion.

The only way to find out what the *Nike Air*, *Max Air* and *Zoom Air* technologies are about, we discovered, is to go to another section of the vast Nike.com website, which is a Flash representation of a metaphorical shoe shop with images of shoes that feature the different kinds of technology. After selecting *Nike Air*, *Max Air* or *Zoom Air* navigation buttons near the top of the page, a strip above them provides a brief definition of each type of technology. *Air* is defined as 'compressed air that sets the standard for cushioning', *Max Air* as 'a large volume of air that provides maximum cushioning' and *Zoom Air* as 'high pressure air that provides responsive, low profile cushioning'.

There is much more to be said about the lack of clarity in the explanation of the *Air*, *Max Air* and *Zoom Air* technologies, but let us now focus on the overall ShopNike.com content structure as represented in the large navigation tree, and on the problems that users of the site may encounter when navigating it. When analysing the site's non-linear structure, we took several major issues into consideration, all related to our attempt to make sense of the classification of Nike products while browsing through the site. At the same time, we kept in mind the more specific goal of buying a pair of quality basketball shoes for which the site is designed. Browsing through the covert translation of the enormous tree, we realized that there were groups, or classes, of items that were presented as if they were at the same hierarchic level but really belonged to different categories that were based on different classification criteria. Some groups were very general categories of items, such as *all footwear*, *all apparel*, etc. Others were specific to different kinds of sport. Yet others were specialty items – for example, items branded with Michael Jordan's name or items that the consumer could customize, etc. To avoid confusion, a superordinate level of structure should have been inserted containing the new *general items*, *sport items* and *specialty items* nodes, and elevating the existing *sport culture* and *clearance items* nodes to this superordinate level. The redesign of this part of the website's structure shown in Figure 6.11 incorporates this idea.

As we have already mentioned, we also realized that the all-encompassing tree was related by network relations to a comparison table of shoe design features. This comparison table enabled, or rather should enable, the shopper to compare the alternative basketball shoes in terms of product design, details and price.

Another major consideration we came up against when perusing ShopNike.com had to do with the role of technology in the overall classification system. We noticed that the Nike proprietary technology, especially *Nike Air* (which consists of air-cushioned soles), features prominently both on ShopNike.com and on the other sections of the overall Nike site. A large image of an Air Max 360 running shoe occupies the main portion of the ShopNike home page, combined with the slogan *More Air, More World*. It has a direct network link to the shoe's covert table page and an opportunity to buy directly without having to browse through the tree. At the same time, there is a network link, as we have seen, from the *Product Technology* description on the shoes'

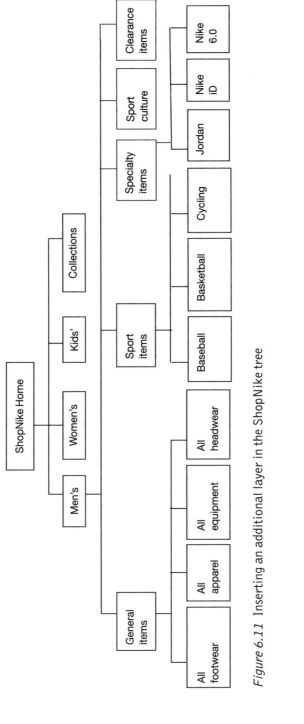

*Figure 6.11* Inserting an additional layer in the ShopNike tree

covert table page to a pop-up window with images and fairly detailed, although confused, explanations of different kinds of Nike Air technology. We surmised then that Nike Air technology forms an important part of Nike marketing strategy and should figure as one of the main criteria for classifying, or identifying, the kind of shoes that shoppers may be interested in buying. And we concluded that it should therefore be placed at a fairly high level of the classification tree.

There is of course the *Air Everywhere* button, close to the top of the overall tree. But it only leads to shoes with Max Air technology, even though this is only one kind of Nike Air technology, the others being Air and Zoom Air. In addition, Nike Air is not the only proprietary technology that Nike have developed. About twenty years ago, the company designed Nike Shox – columns of rubber in the sole functioning as shock absorbers. This invention is still popular as can be inferred from the number of different kinds of Nike Shox sport shoes on ShopNike.com, as well as from the network links in the second translations of the Nike Shox shoes' tables leading to pop-up windows similar to those with Nike Air illustrations and explanations (see Figure 6.10). Then there are other technologies that Nike uses to build quality shoes which are either not proprietary or not distinctive enough to deserve special mention, such as those used to make cycling shoes.

Based on the obvious importance of Nike Air and to a lesser extent of Nike Shox to Nike strategy, we believe that *Technology* should be a node directly dependent on the *All footwear* node (see Figures 6.8 and 6.11). The technology attribute would then apply to all footwear categories. We believe that the Nike target audience would agree with us, given how much they have been exposed especially to Nike Air on the Nike website and in Nike advertisements. This means that, in our redesign, Nike technology and Nike footwear types are two simultaneous attributes of *All footwear*, which are best represented as two satellites of an *All footwear* nucleus, as in Figure 6.12.

The Nike technology part of the navigation tree can now form another navigation path through the ShopNike.com site, departing from the *All footwear* node. Taking this path, the user can decide to look for footwear with either Nike Air or Nike Shox technology. If s/he decides to look for Nike Air shoes, this leads to the choice of either footwear with Air or Max Air or Zoom Air technology. If, for instance, a user then decides to narrow the search to Max Air sport shoes only, s/he would then be led to either basketball or running shoes with Max Air, because these are the only two kinds of sport shoes that have that kind of technology. If s/he then decided on basketball shoes, s/he would be presented with the choice of Nike Air Max 360 BBall and Nike Air Max 180 BB (men). The Nike technology part of the navigation tree is represented in Figure 6.13.

In order to make the choice, the user would need to compare the two kinds of shoes in terms of their various attributes to see which one would suit him/her better, which suggests a comparison table (see Figure 6.14).

Instead of repeating, below *Max Air*, the *Basketball* and *Running*, and *Nike Air Max 360 BBall* and *Nike Air Max 180 BB (men)* nodes, which are already represented in the *Sport footwear* part of the tree, the *Max Air* node can be directly linked

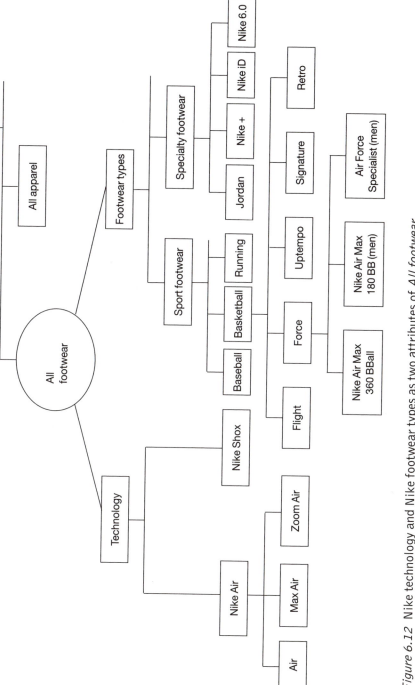

*Figure 6.12* Nike technology and Nike footwear types as two attributes of *All footwear*

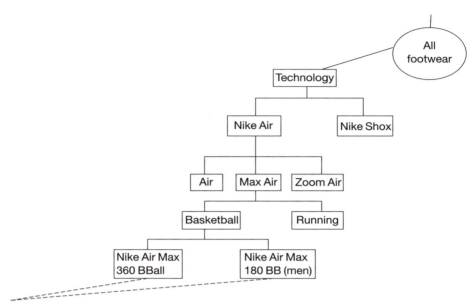

Leading to a table that compares Nike Air Max 360 BBall and Nike Air Max 180 BB (men), i.e. Max Air Basketball shoes.

*Figure 6.13* Nike technology part of the ShopNike navigation tree

to the Nike Air Max 360 BB and Nike Air Max 180 BB (men) nodes by network rela-tions. These, in turn, are linked to their comparison tables. This alternative is presented in Figure 6.15.

From the point of view of conceptual organization, the two alternatives are simply different solutions to the same problem, the first being probably better for display purposes. The second translation of this alternative solution would of course be different, with network links taking the place of covert tree links on the *Max Air* page.

## Second translation of ShopNike

The complex non-linear model of the ShopNike.com structure is of course just a conceptual model that shows how the various pieces of content are related to one another semantically. In this section we will present a translation of the semantic structure into screens and navigation systems. The website is very different from the other website we will analyse and redesign, the Calvary Presbyterian Church website, but, as we will demonstrate, the same hierarchy of periodicity approach can be used to redesign both.

| | Upper feature/function | Strap feature/function | Sole feature/function | Outsole feature/function | Colour | Price |
|---|---|---|---|---|---|---|
| **Nike Air Max 360 BBall** | Layered full-grain leather and premium synthetic/delivers a supportive, protective fit for harnessing the power of the force player | Well-crafted, supportive strap/improves protection and lockdown | Full-length engineered maximum Air-Sole unit/provides cutting edge cushioning, ride, and heel-to-toe transition | Solid and translucent rubber combination outsole with ribbed herringbone pattern/promises max traction and forefoot flexibility | White/Hoop Orange/Black | $160.00 |
| **Nike Air Max 180 BB (men)** | Premium synthetic and full-grain leather upper/provides incredible comfort and a protective fit | Removable strap/offers enhanced ankle support | Double-lasted Phylon midsole, forefoot Zoom Air unit, and maximum heel Air-Sole unit/deliver incredible cushioning and responsiveness | Solid and translucent rubber outsole with ribbed herringbone pattern/offers maximum traction and forefoot flexibility | White/Black/Varsity Royal | $120.00 |

*Figure 6.14* A table comparing basketball shoes featuring Max Air technology

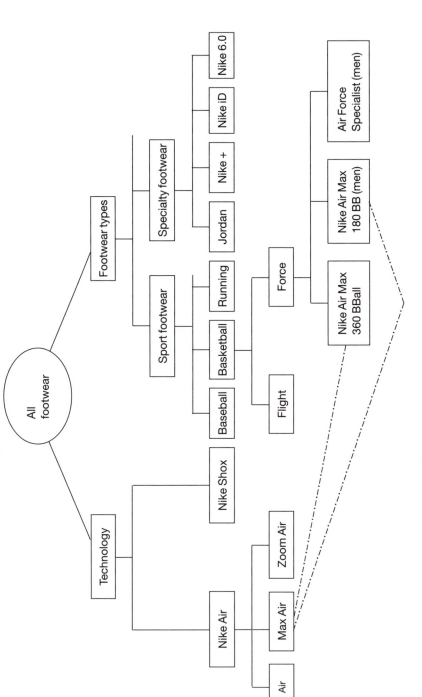

*Figure 6.15* An alternative representation of the Nike technology part of the ShopNike navigation tree

A key difference between the two websites is the navigation bar that tracks the path of the shopper through the ShopNike.com site structure. This is a feature of the original ShopNike.com site and we have kept it (albeit in a slightly modified form) because the site is complex, with many layers of structure, and it is good for the shopper to know where on the site s/he is at any particular point in time. This is particularly true of our redesigned site since, following the hierarchy of periodicity approach, we have done away with the covert translation of the big tree on the left side of the original site. There are three reasons why we do not think this tree is necessary. First of all, the shopper's progress through the site is kept track of by the bar at the top of the page, and clicking on any one of the buttons in the sequence will display the alternatives at that layer of structure. We have also kept a link to the ShopNike. com home page in the top-left corner of every screen, so the top layer of the site's structure is always available. Secondly, as we have seen, not all the semantic relations in the site structure are tree relations. There is, for instance, the star relationship between the *technology* and *types of shoes* satellites on the one hand and the *(all) footwear* nucleus on the other, and star relations are usually translated differently from tree relations. Just indenting them on the left side of the screen does not do justice to their semantic difference. Finally, like many websites whose main semantic structure is a tree, the ShopNike covert tree emulates a book's table of contents. But tables of contents do not usually display levels of structure below that of the chapters (i.e. sections and subsections), even when these are explicitly marked by titles in the actual text. This is no doubt at least in part because tables of contents with too many layers of structure are unwieldy and likely to result in not being able to see the wood for the trees. To give an example, the table of contents of Donald Norman's *The Design of Everyday Things* consists only of chapter headings, and yet each chapter in the text consists of clearly titled sections and subsections. Books aimed at a more academic audience do show more layers of structure in their tables of content. As we have seen, George Lakoff's *Women, Fire and Dangerous Things* has the levels of Book, Part and Chapter. There are, however, only two Books, and only the first has two Parts. This clearly contrasts with the plethora of titles at each hierarchic layer of the ShopNike covert tree.

Figure 6.16 represents the second translation of a particular path through the redesigned ShopNike site. The translation is based on the non-linear ShopNike structure presented in Figures 6.11, 6.12, 6.13 and 6.14 and consists of a sequence of screens, starting with the Home Page and ending with a redesigned translation of the Nike Air Max 360 BBall comparison-table entry (see Figure 6.14). The Home Page consists of an introduction to the whole website and an outline of the topics to be dealt with in the next layer of structure. Navigation buttons condense this outline. The Home Page button in the top-left corner is non-clickable since it is on the Home Page itself. The arrow leading from the *Men's* navigation button represents the link to the relevant next-layer screen.

Each layer of the following screens consists of an expansion of the topics outlined on the previous layer's screens and condensed in the navigation buttons, followed by

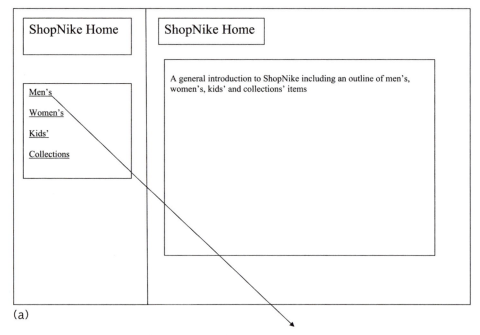

(a)

*Figure 6.16* (a–i) Second translation of a path through a redesigned ShopNike.com

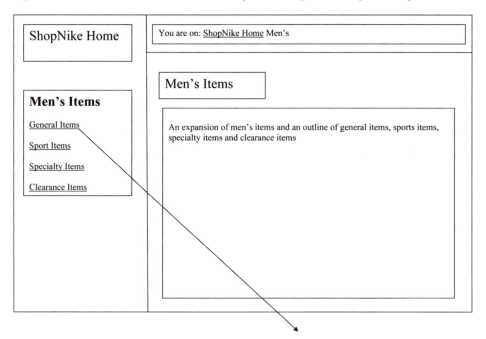

*Figure 6.16* (b)

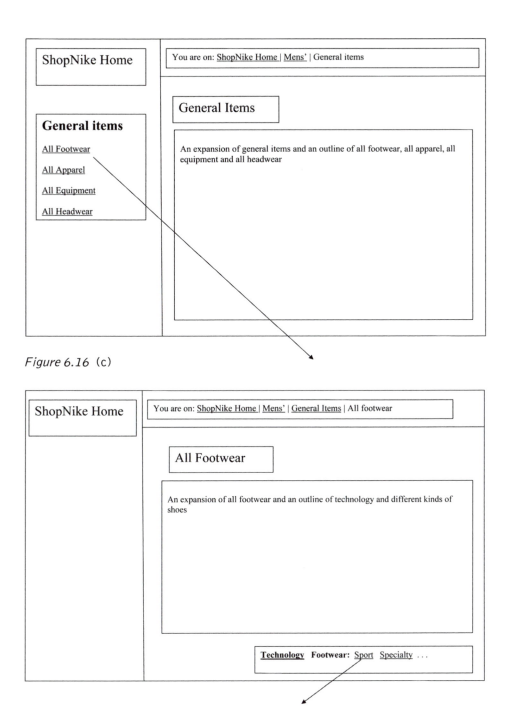

*Figure 6.16* (c)

*Figure 6.16* (d)

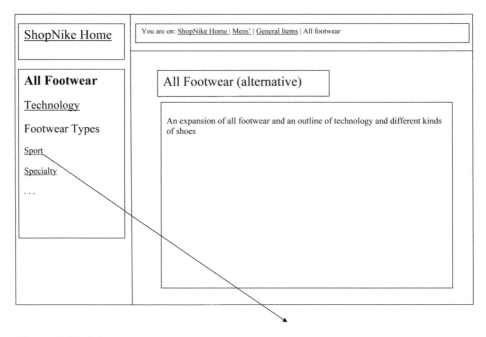

Figure 6.16 (e)

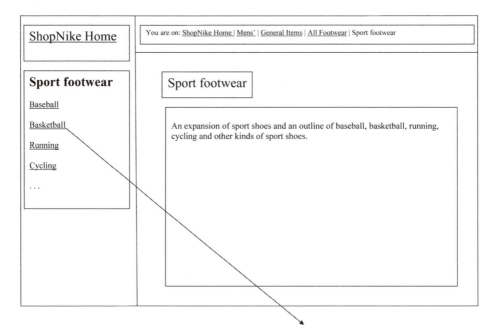

Figure 6.16 (f)

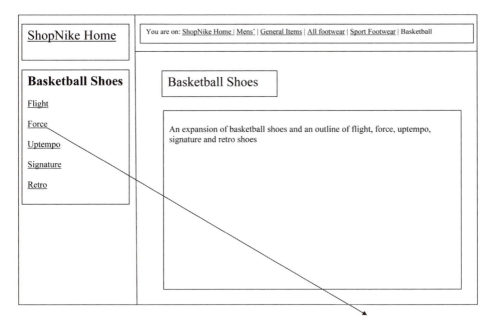

*Figure 6.16* (g)

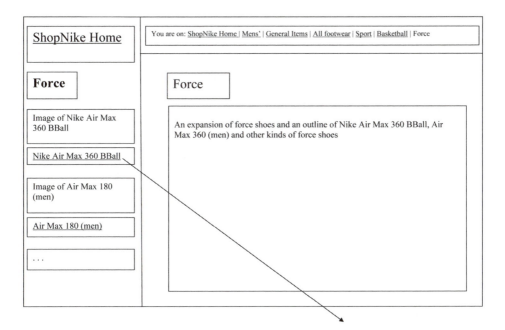

*Figure 6.16* (h)

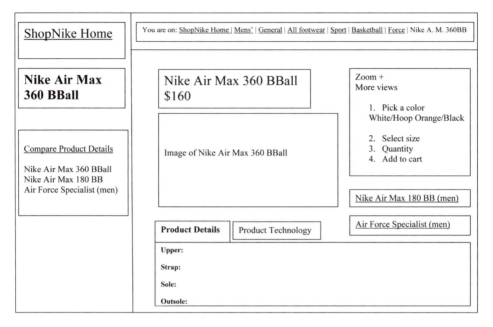

*Figure 6.16* (i)

an outline of the topics at the next-lower layer of the site structure (see Figure 5.1). Apart from the (now clickable) Home Page button, each screen also contains navigation buttons that lead to the next layer of structure and the (non-clickable) title of the current screen. In addition, there is a bar at the top of the page, tracking the place of the current page in the overall website structure. All the buttons on this bar, except that of the current screen, are clickable and lead to the relevant screens. This progress-tracking bar thus looks backwards from the current page to all the previous pages the user has passed through, whereas the navigation bar on the left of the screen looks forward to the next layer of the site's structure.

Two issues remain to be discussed, the position of the navigation buttons on the *All Footwear* page, and the last page, which is the covert translation of a row in a table concerned with Nike Air Max 360 BBall. The position of the navigation buttons at the bottom of the *All Footwear* page follows the star second translation conventions we established earlier (see Figure 4.29). It does, however, break with the pattern set up by the position of the navigation buttons on the previous (and following) pages and might therefore jar a little on the user. An alternative version could place the buttons in the same position as in the other covert tree navigation. This would create a different problem, however, since the usual way of expressing hierarchy through the size and type of font would not apply. There would be two buttons at the same hierarchic level: *Technology* and *Shoe Types*, breaking up the previously established hierarchical pattern of a superordinate and its subordinates. Having a non-clickable

*Shoe Types* superordinate would not be a problem since this is one way of skipping a layer of structure which does not have enough content to make it worthwhile. All things considered, we would opt for the first solution. Deciding which of the two would be more successful with shoppers would, however, have to be tested.

As for the last page of this particular path through the ShopNike.com site, its major component is a redesigned Nike Air Max 360 BBall row in the table comparing the three different kinds of *Force* shoes (see Figure 6.9). The covert translation of the row consists of the shoe's image and title, *Nike Air Max 360 BBall*, and of the attributes in terms of which it can be compared with the other *Force* shoe alternatives (upper, strap, sole, outsole and colour). We have moved the shoe title to the more usual place, above the image, and the *Zoom +* and *More views* buttons to where the title originally was. This causes the product attributes to stand out better, and makes it easier to compare with other products. The comparison has further been facilitated by adding the other two shoes' buttons on the right side of the page, and a link to the table on the left. The shoes and their attributes appear next to each other in the table, and so can all be seen at a glance. The *Product Technology* button at the bottom of the page leads to a description in which the technology attributes have been prominently marked, similar to the *Product Details* attributes.

In the original design, comparing the shoes was rather difficult. There were no buttons on the page to lead directly to the pages with the other two products. To see them and to read about their attributes, one would have to go back to the *Force* page (see Figure 6.6) and click on the other shoes' navigation buttons. This process might make it difficult to keep the previous shoe's attributes in mind, especially since they were described in a way that did not make them stand out, and in rather different wordings.

We cannot emphasize enough how important it is for shoppers to be able to compare the shoes at this stage of their journey through the ShopNike site. They have finally arrived at the last three alternatives and now have to make a choice. And without being able to properly compare the available options, it is impossible to make an informed choice. It may well be that Nike thinks their target audience already has sufficient knowledge to make a choice and does not need to access a page with explicit comparisons. If so, this would be, we feel, a complacent attitude. Offering the possibility of explicit comparison would serve shoppers better.

We will now present the second translation of another path through the ShopNike. com website. This path concerns Nike technology. It begins with the Nike technology page and ends with the Nike Air Max 360 BBall page, and it is shown in Figure 6.17. The relevant part of the overall site's non-linear structure was diagrammed in Figures 6.12 and 6.13.

It could be argued that there are too many clicks on the path to the final selection of the shoes. We would counter by saying that the added clarity is well worth the extra clicks for customers who want to inform themselves about Nike shoes and plan to spend a not inconsiderable amount of money on buying a pair. Good quality sport shoes are an expensive, high-involvement product, consisting of many technologically

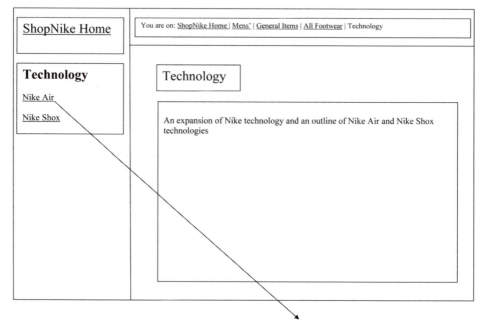

| ShopNike Home | You are on: <u>ShopNike Home</u> | <u>Mens'</u> | <u>General Items</u> | <u>All Footwear</u> | Technology |
| --- | --- |
| **Technology**<br><br><u>Nike Air</u><br><br><u>Nike Shox</u> | Technology<br><br>An expansion of Nike technology and an outline of Nike Air and Nike Shox technologies |

*Figure 6.17* (a) A second translation of the Nike Technology path through a redesigned ShopNike.com

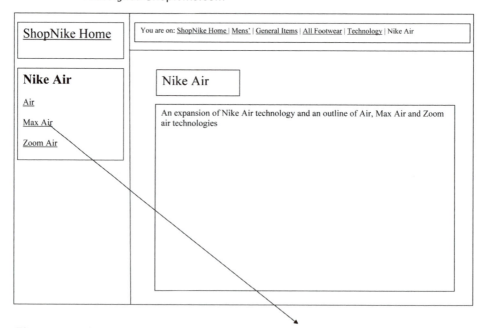

| ShopNike Home | You are on: <u>ShopNike Home</u> | <u>Mens'</u> | <u>General Items</u> | <u>All Footwear</u> | <u>Technology</u> | Nike Air |
| --- | --- |
| **Nike Air**<br><br><u>Air</u><br><br><u>Max Air</u><br><br><u>Zoom Air</u> | Nike Air<br><br>An expansion of Nike Air technology and an outline of Air, Max Air and Zoom air technologies |

*Figure 6.17* (b)

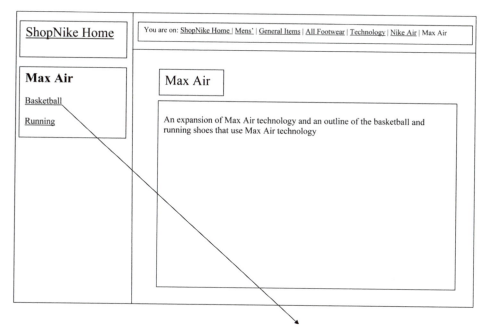

*Figure 6.17* (c)

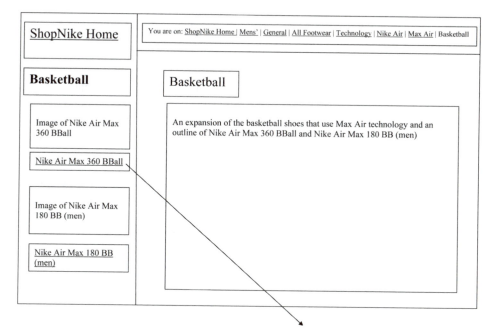

*Figure 6.17* (d)

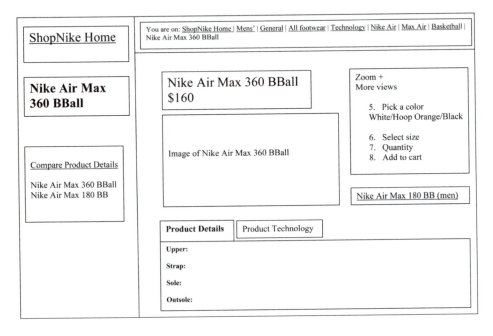

*Figure 6.17* (e)

sophisticated components. Potential customers are therefore likely to want as much information as possible before making a purchase.

Let us now consider the periodic structure of the second translation's paths through ShopNike.com. It could be argued that ShopNike.com is just a site for selecting shoes and that it should do no more than that. This depends on the firm's strategy. We do not exactly know what Nike's strategy for ShopNike.com was, but we do know that the site provides a good deal of fairly detailed technological information in the pop-up windows that are linked to the Product Technology descriptions on the shoes' final pages. So technology is clearly important. For this reason we believe that this information should be elevated in the overall site hierarchy and described and illustrated on the pages dealing with Nike technology. As we already discussed, customers are likely to appreciate solid information on high-involvement products such as basketball, running, and other shoes. And this applies not just to the description of the shoes on the last page, but also to information about the nodes that are higher in the overall site structure, such as Nike sport shoes in general, basketball shoes, and so on.

We would also argue that the periodic structure we have proposed emulates the structure of the discourse of shop associates (see Martinec 2002 for hierarchy of periodicity in dialogue) and contains, more or less, the kind of information they would pass on to customers in actual Nike stores. As Hanson (2001) explains, online shopping can be made easier and more user-friendly by emulating real-world shopping experiences. We believe that our redesign is closer than the original ShopNike site to how a shopping interaction may actually occur in the real world, although it could certainly be improved by an analysis of real shopping discourse samples.

It could finally be argued that the information we have incorporated in our redesign can be found elsewhere in the larger Nike.com website of which ShopNike.com forms a part. It is true that some of the information we included in our redesign also appears in the Flash sections of Nike.com. But not everyone would be willing to wait for the Flash movie in the centre of the home page to download and not everyone would be interested in the image-heavy sections that can be accessed from the home page. Flash introductions play a role in strategies of impressing young target audiences, but what if the customer is a parent intending to buy a new pair of Nikes for their offspring? In any case, we believe that ShopNike.com should be a self-contained section of the site, since, once on it, it is not easy for customers to switch to the other, Flash sections of the overall site and look for more information about a specific node in the path through the ShopNike.com section they are following.

## First and second translation redesigns of the Calvary Presbyterian Church website

The second website we will analyse and redesign is the website of the Calvary Presbyterian Church in San Francisco, California. The strategy that informs this website is very different from that of ShopNike.com. It seeks to provide as much information as possible about the church itself and the community that congregates around it, including all the different kinds of activities the community members are involved in. Quite appropriately, the non-linear model behind the main part of the website is therefore that of a star, with the church and the community as the nucleus in the centre, and the various activities as the satellites on the margins. Some of these satellites are simultaneously the superordinate nodes of classification trees.

Landing on the Calvary home page presents visitors to the site with a photo of the church, a welcome and a brief introduction to the church community, as well as an invitation to join the community for worship. The times and dates of the gatherings are specified and so is the church location. There is also an *Upcoming Events* column on the left side of the home page with a list of events that will take place in the near future and links to pages with further information. Above the photo is a navigation bar leading to a variety of topics: *Ministries and Fellowships, Calendar, Staff, History, Music, Sermons* and *Photo Gallery*. The *Calvary Presbyterian Church* title is above the navigation bar. The home page is represented in Figure 6.18 (see also Figure 4.28).

Clicking on the navigation bar buttons leads to pages with more information on the relevant topics. For example, the Staff button leads to the Calvary staff curricula, and the Ministries and Fellowships button leads to a *Calvary Activities* page with a very short introduction and a number of links organized hierarchically under the categories of *Education, Fellowship, Serving* and *Worship* (see Figure 6.19).

## Calvary Presbyterian Church

| Home | Ministries and Fellowships | Calendar | Staff | History | Music | Sermons | Photo Gallery |
|---|---|---|---|---|---|---|---|

**Upcoming Events**

Saturday, August 26
Bike Ride & Barbecue
(see Calendar for more info)

September 16–Oct 11
Calvary Connects
Building Bridges in our Community

Presbyterians Against Torture

Calvary Presbyterian Church
image

**Welcome to Calvary Presbyterian Church**
We are a community of believers united by faith, scripture, and the constitution of our denomination committed to calling people to Christ and encouraging one another in faith through worship, education, fellowship, and service.

**Worship with us**
Calvary is located at the corner of Jackson and Fillmore Streets in San Francisco's Pacific Heights neighborhood. The members, friends and visitors of Calvary gather for worship at 8:45 and 11:00 each Sunday morning. Church School and opportunities for adult education are offered between the services. A coffee hour follows each service of worship.

Parking is available on Sundays at the Newcomer School, east of the church on Jackson. Additional validated parking at CPMC Hospital garage on Clay, between Fillmore and Webster. Muni lines #22 Fillmore, #24 Divisadero and #3 Jackson serve this intersection as well.

**Address:**
Calvary Presbyterian Church
2515 Fillmore St.
San Francisco, CA 94115
Driving directions available on map link : [ map ]

**Phone:** 415 346 3832
**Fax:** 415 346 1436

Wheelchair accessible

*Figure 6.18* Calvary Presbyterian Church home page

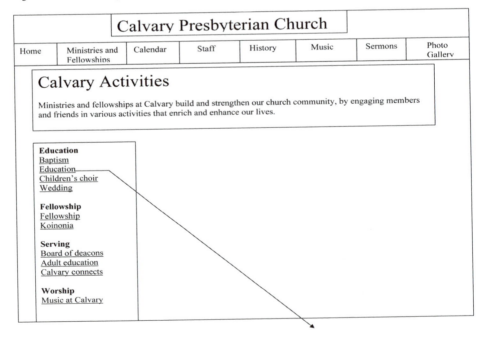

*Figure 6.19* Ministries and Fellowships/Calvary Activities page

The links, in turn, lead to pages at the third layer of structure, where a short introduction may be provided with more links leading to further information in the fourth layer. An example is the *Education at Calvary* page represented in Figure 6.20.

The Music button on the home page navigation bar leads to a page where a considerable amount of information about music at Calvary is given, without any links except to download music produced by one of the Calvary choirs (see Figure 6.21).

The Sermons button on the home page leads to a page titled *Recent Sermons* with a link to the *Sermons Archive* and other links to more recent sermons (see Figure 6.22).

We hope these examples will suffice to create a picture of the site in the reader's mind. Let us now consider the complex non-linear model we extracted from the site. As we discussed in Chapter 1, existing websites are most commonly built by following the design of non-linear storyboards, or 'wire frames'. These are generally chunks of text and images that represent screens, connected by lines that represent navigation links. So when we extract the non-linear structure of an existing new media product, we in fact, more than anything, map out its navigation structure, considering the navigation buttons' titles to stand for the linked pages. The non-linear model of the Calvary Presbyterian Church website we have extracted in this way is represented in Figure 6.23.

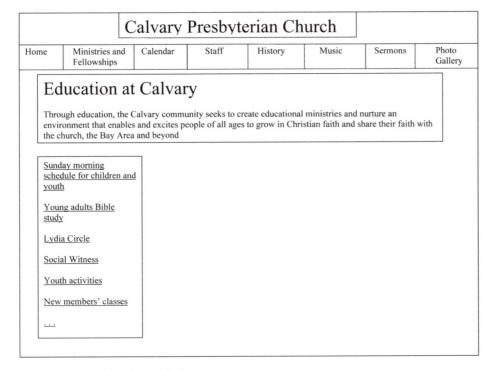

*Figure 6.20* Education at Calvary page

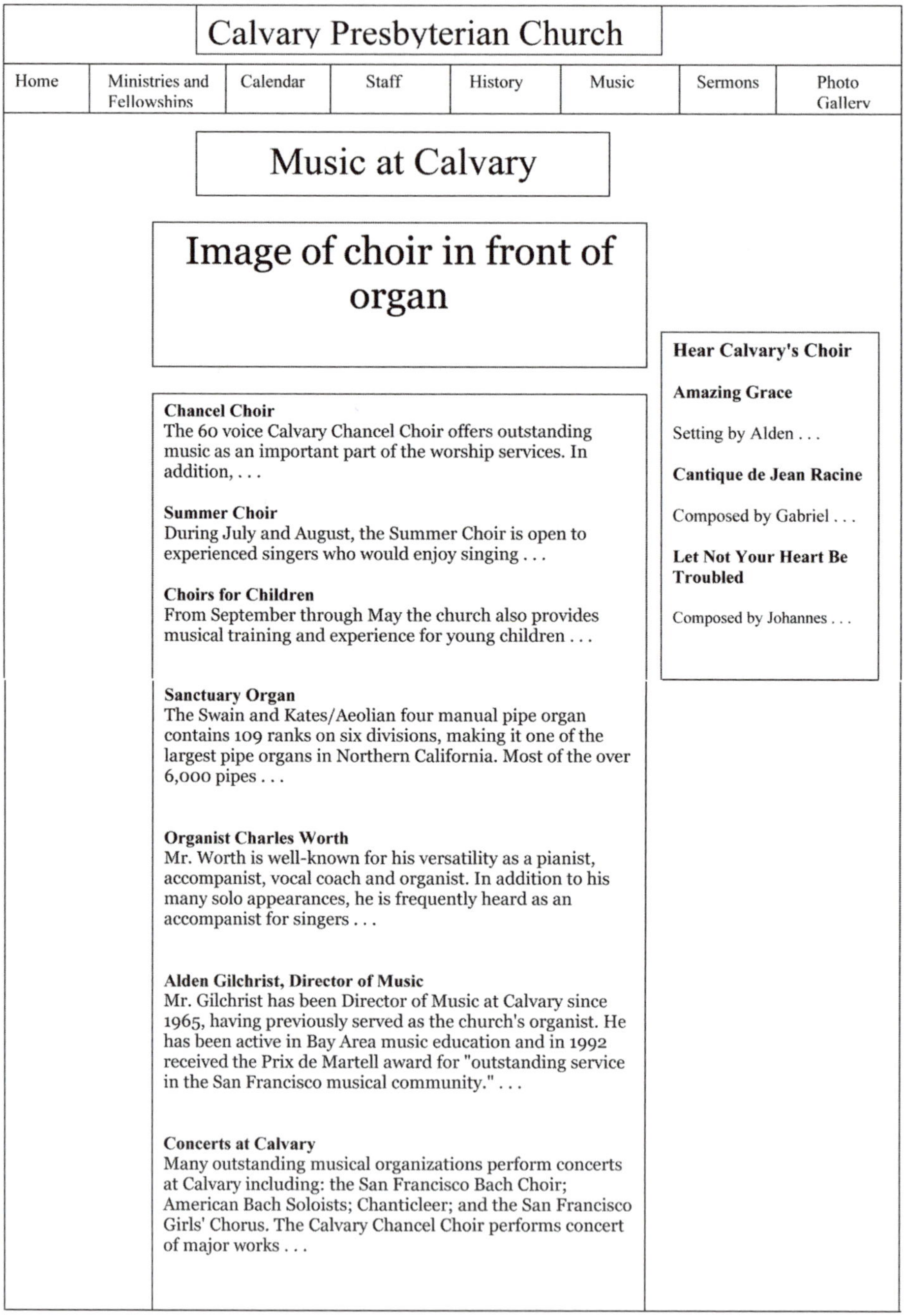

| Calvary Presbyterian Church | | | | | | | |
|---|---|---|---|---|---|---|---|
| Home | Ministries and Fellowships | Calendar | Staff | History | Music | Sermons | Photo Gallery |

## Music at Calvary

Image of choir in front of organ

**Hear Calvary's Choir**

**Amazing Grace**

Setting by Alden . . .

**Cantique de Jean Racine**

Composed by Gabriel . . .

**Let Not Your Heart Be Troubled**

Composed by Johannes . . .

**Chancel Choir**
The 60 voice Calvary Chancel Choir offers outstanding music as an important part of the worship services. In addition, . . .

**Summer Choir**
During July and August, the Summer Choir is open to experienced singers who would enjoy singing . . .

**Choirs for Children**
From September through May the church also provides musical training and experience for young children . . .

**Sanctuary Organ**
The Swain and Kates/Aeolian four manual pipe organ contains 109 ranks on six divisions, making it one of the largest pipe organs in Northern California. Most of the over 6,000 pipes . . .

**Organist Charles Worth**
Mr. Worth is well-known for his versatility as a pianist, accompanist, vocal coach and organist. In addition to his many solo appearances, he is frequently heard as an accompanist for singers . . .

**Alden Gilchrist, Director of Music**
Mr. Gilchrist has been Director of Music at Calvary since 1965, having previously served as the church's organist. He has been active in Bay Area music education and in 1992 received the Prix de Martell award for "outstanding service in the San Francisco musical community." . . .

**Concerts at Calvary**
Many outstanding musical organizations perform concerts at Calvary including: the San Francisco Bach Choir; American Bach Soloists; Chanticleer; and the San Francisco Girls' Chorus. The Calvary Chancel Choir performs concert of major works . . .

*Figure 6.21* Music at Calvary page

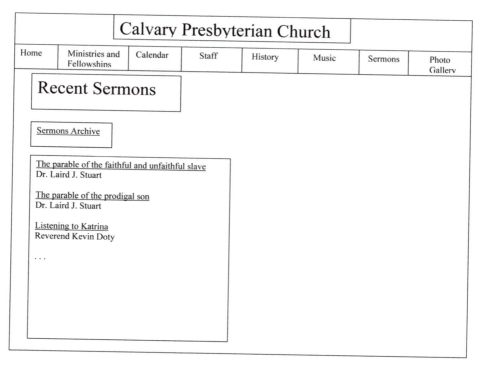

*Figure 6.22* Recent Sermons page

After extracting the complex non-linear model that underlies the existing Calvary website, we will now take the second step and analyse the content of the web pages to see if the non-linear structure we have extracted from the website is appropriate for the non-linear structure of the content. We will start by analysing the content of the home page (see Figure 6.18). After analysing its content for non-linear models, we will compare the result with the existing navigation buttons that form the first layer of navigation. According to our generic structure principle, these navigation buttons should condense the main topics of the home page content. The content of the navigation buttons should then in turn be expanded in the content of the pages at the second layer of website structure. Our non-linear model of the content of the Calvary home page is presented in Figure 6.24.

The structure of complex non-linear models is to some extent a matter of interpretation. As we saw in Chapter 3, this is mostly due to choices in the level of detail of the analyses, which, in turn, is given by the purposes of the sites' designers. The Calvary website already has a purpose – that of the original designer – which we have tried to respect. When analysing the home page, we thus took a simpler approach and decided our analysis would be guided by the principle that an appropriate level of detail should result in navigation buttons which, when expanded, yield pages with sufficiently worthwhile content.

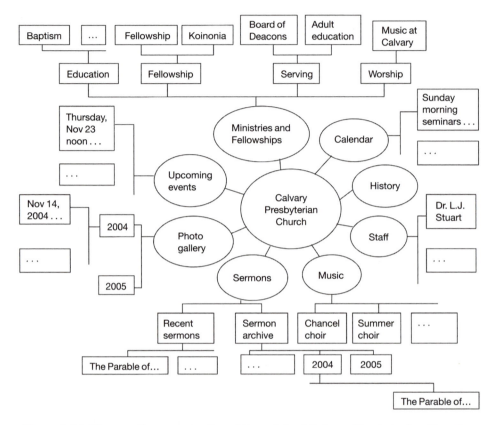

*Figure 6.23* The non-linear semantics of the original Calvary Presbyterian Church website

We could have analysed the site in a greater level of detail; however, the above-mentioned criterion provides a valid check on the depth of analysis. Since the analysis is semantic, dealing with meanings rather than wordings, we have at times reformulated the original words to better capture the relationships between the concepts in the text. The complex non-linear model that maps out the semantics of the text on the home page consists mostly of star relations, the overall star having at times just two, and other times three layers of structure.

According to our periodic-structure model of new media products, the home page (HP) should outline the contents of the whole product and the main topics of the outline should be condensed in the first layer of the product's navigation. Let us then compare the topics and the buttons as they are in the existing design:

1. Although 'Community' is a prominent part of the HP's semantic field and should therefore have a navigation button of its own, leading to a page (or pages) at the

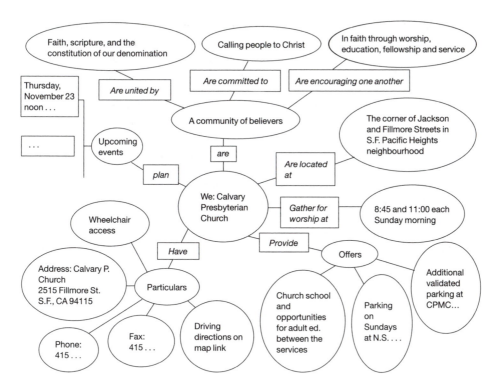

*Figure 6.24* A non-linear model analysis of the Calvary Presbyterian Church home
page

second layer of the website structure, there is no navigation button with that label
on the HP navigation bar.

2. All three satellites that depend on the *a community of believers* nucleus are
   related to one or another of the first-layer navigation buttons (see Figure 6.18).
   *Faith, scripture, and the constitution of our denomination* is related to the
   *sermons* button; *calling people to Christ* is related to the *sermons* and *ministries
   and fellowships* buttons; and *in faith through worship, education, fellowship and
   service* is related to the *sermons* and *ministries and fellowships* buttons. An
   important part of the last node, namely *education,* however, is not represented in
   the navigation. It is about the church school and opportunities for adult education which are mentioned in the second paragraph of the HP and in one of the
   nodes dependent on the *offers* nucleus.

3. The location of the Church is obviously quite important since it is mentioned
   no less than three times, as represented in the nodes *the corner of Jackson and*

*Fillmore Streets in S.F. Pacific Heights neighborhood, Address: Calvary Presby-terian Church, 2515 Fillmore St., San Francisco, CA 94115,* and *driving direc-tions on map link.* There is, however, not much to be said about the Church location apart from what is already on the home page. The driving directions do not need a whole second-layer page to themselves and they are not of the same level of importance as the other navigation bar topics. A network link to the driving directions and the map, as provided in the original design, would have sufficed.

4. The *8:45 and 11:00 each Sunday morning* node is related to the current *calendar* primary-layer navigation button.

5. The *We: Calvary Presbyterian Church* nucleus and its *a community of believers* satellite are related to the current *staff* button.

6. In order to keep the navigation design consistent, we would include an *upcoming events* button in the same navigation bar with others. This would free the amount of horizontal space on the home page, which means that the user would not have to scroll to read the whole text.

7. *Music* has its own button on the current navigation bar, although it is not mentioned in the text of the HP. We would argue for either a brief mention or for leaving its navigation button for the next-lower layer of navigation. The choice would depend on how important a part of the church's strategy music is. It may be considered highly important if it plays a role in recruiting new members for the church community, in which case the first option would apply. Otherwise the second option might be a better solution.

8. In the original design, there is a navigation button called *staff*. We would include the church staff under the more all-encompassing *community*, and deal with it at the next layer of structure. It may be part of the Calvary strategy to present their staff as a major selling point and thus place them in a more elevated position in the website structure. They are, however, not mentioned on the home page and are certainly a part, albeit an important one, of our new *community* category.

9. There is also a button called *photo gallery* in the original navigation bar. Photos are not mentioned on the home page, which is probably correct since the HP is not the right place for mentioning them. They certainly do add interest to the site, which may be part of the designer's strategy, but they are not at the same level of importance as the other topics in the navigation bar, and they lack the immediate practical importance of, for instance, the driving directions. Hence they should be placed at a lower layer of the website structure.

10. The *history* navigation button does probably make sense as part of the first-layer navigation bar, since most organizations pride themselves on their history. The Calvary Presbyterian Church is no exception here.

Based on the above analysis of the non-linear semantics of the HP content and on our periodic-structure based approach, we have redesigned the Calvary Presbyterian Church home page as in Figure 6.25.

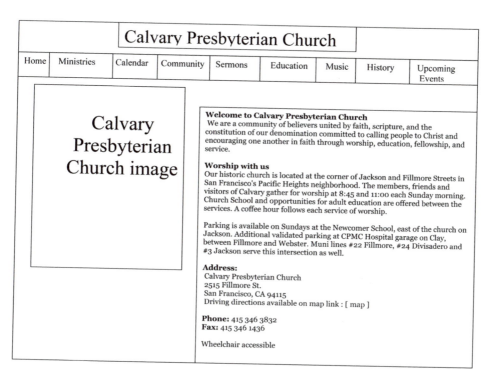

*Figure 6.25* Redesign of the Calvary Presbyterian Church home page

In our redesign, we kept as close as possible to the original home page design. There are, however, other ways of redesigning the home page. The non-linear model behind the home page and the first layer of navigation is a star, and translating it the way we have done uses the second translation conventions of creating a covert star in navigation. There is a title at the top of the page, which translates the star's nucleus, and a horizontal navigation bar below it whose buttons translate the information that is in the satellite nodes. We have not carried out any second translation of the star into interface, but instead kept the interface more or less as it was in the original design (except for removing the list of *Upcoming Events* and using the space for displaying the church image).

A more radical redesign may use an overt star in the interface as a navigation device. An iconic, overt translation of the semantics behind the site may look something like in Figure 6.26.

The overt star in this redesign may be seen as motivated by religious paintings like Murillo's Madonna (see Figure 2.14) and could therefore be considered appropriate for a Church website. The image in the nucleus of the star is clickable and leads to a page with the information which, in the original version of the site, is on the home page. The image could include the words *about us* in white, transparent letters, or use some other method to indicate that it is a navigation button.

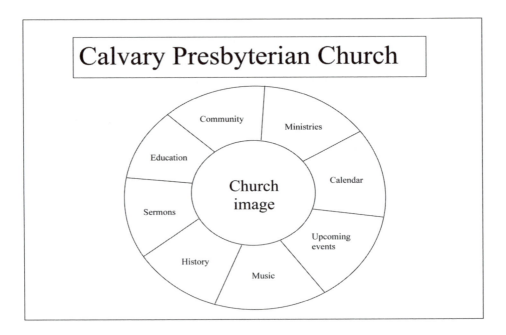

*Figure 6.26* An overt star redesign of the Calvary Presbyterian Church home page

Let us now move to redesigning the second layer of the Calvary Church site structure. The original design is highly inconsistent. The *Music at Calvary* page, for example, is full of complex text. Yet, apart from the title of the page and the paragraph headings (the print conventions for representing a covert tree), none of the non-linear semantics of the content is made explicit. This contrasts with, say, the *Calvary Activities* page that appears after clicking on the *Ministries and Fellowships* navigation button. Apart from the two-line introduction, there is no text, but only the covert translation of a classification tree, with *Calvary Activities* as the superordinate, and *education, fellowship, serving* and *worship* as subordinates which, in turn, become superordinates for the next-lower layer of subordinates (*baptism, education*, etc.).

Following the hierarchy of periodicity approach, we would argue that each page should have some text to expand the content condensed in the navigation button leading to it, and an outline of topics that themselves get condensed in navigation buttons leading to other pages, in which those topics are treated in more detail. From this perspective, the *Calvary Activities* page has too little text, whereas the *Music at Calvary* page has too few links (in fact none, if one excludes the links for music downloads).

We will thus redesign both pages to make them more consistent. Let us begin with the *Music at Calvary* page, whose content is quite complex. In order to preserve the more or less equal chunking of content across the different website structure layers, we first extracted the non-linear model that structures its semantics, which can be translated into consistently designed pages. The non-linear model is in Figure 6.27.

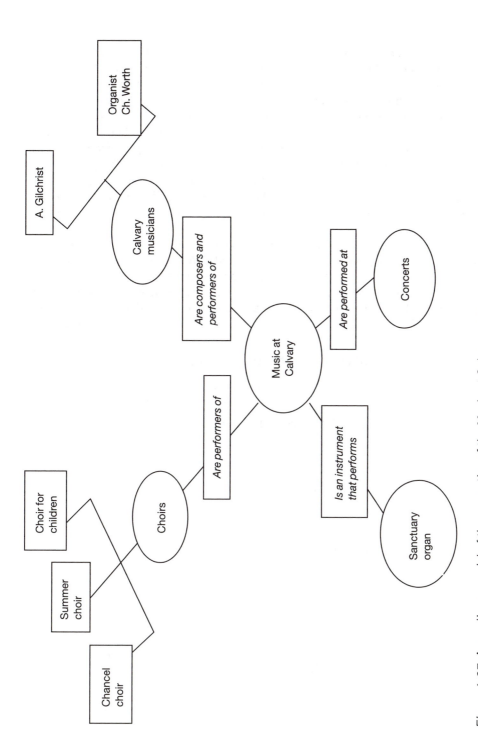

*Figure 6.27* A non-linear model of the semantics of the Music at Calvary page

As we said above, we try to keep as close as possible to the original designers' strategy when redesigning websites, so what guides the level of detail of our analysis is the principle that we focus on only such content as is worthwhile enough to justify setting up a web page. The non-linear model which structures the semantics of the *Music at Calvary* page is a star with trees connected to two satellites. The topics that form the satellites are all related to the nuclear *Music at Calvary* but in a star rather than a tree manner, as the existing website would seem to suggest, and two of them have subtopics. These two satellites, quite appropriately, have enough content to fill a page, whereas the other two do not, and will therefore in the second translation be grouped together on one page at the third layer of structure of the redesigned website. Figures 6.28, 6.29, 6.30 and 6.31 show the second translation of the non-linear model.

The layout of the page in Figure 6.28 includes an image of a choir performing a concert, as in the original version of the *Music at Calvary* page. The text below contains a general introduction that briefly summarizes all the topics related to *Music at Calvary* (the different choirs, the sanctuary organ, etc.). Finally, the navigation buttons at the bottom of the page condense the introduction and lead to pages at the next-lower layer of structure that expand the topics (see Figures 6.29, 6.30 and 6.31).

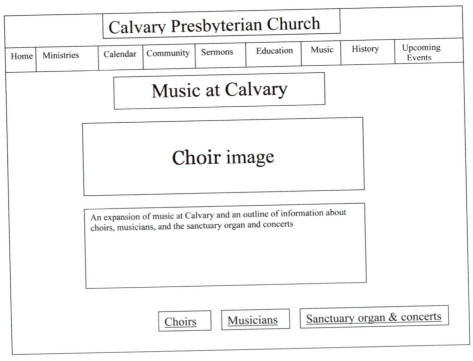

*Figure 6.28* A redesigned Music at Calvary page (second layer of Calvary Church website)

| Home | Ministries | Calendar | Community | Sermons | Education | Music | History | Upcoming Events |

# Calvary Presbyterian Church

## Calvary's Choirs

**Chancel Choir**
The 60 voice Calvary Chancel Choir offers outstanding music as an important part of the worship services. In addition, . . .

**Summer Choir**
During July and August, the Summer Choir is open to experienced singers who would enjoy singing for the 11:00 a.m. worship service for one or more weeks. Rehearsals are on Sundays at 10:00 a.m

**Choir for Children**
From September through May the church also provides musical training and experience for young children from kindergarten through the seventh grade.

**Hear Calvary's Choir**

**Amazing Grace**

Setting by Alden . . .

**Cantique de Jean Racine**

Composed by Gabriel . . .

**Let Not Your Heart Be Troubled**

Composed by Johannes . . .

In May 1998, Mr. Gilchrist's musical setting to the biblical story of Daniel was performed by members of all three Calvary choirs.

*Figure 6.29* Calvary Choirs page

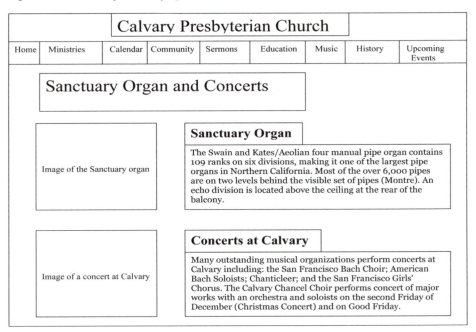

| Home | Ministries | Calendar | Community | Sermons | Education | Music | History | Upcoming Events |

# Calvary Presbyterian Church

## Sanctuary Organ and Concerts

Image of the Sanctuary organ

### Sanctuary Organ

The Swain and Kates/Aeolian four manual pipe organ contains 109 ranks on six divisions, making it one of the largest pipe organs in Northern California. Most of the over 6,000 pipes are on two levels behind the visible set of pipes (Montre). An echo division is located above the ceiling at the rear of the balcony.

Image of a concert at Calvary

### Concerts at Calvary

Many outstanding musical organizations perform concerts at Calvary including: the San Francisco Bach Choir; American Bach Soloists; Chanticleer; and the San Francisco Girls' Chorus. The Calvary Chancel Choir performs concert of major works with an orchestra and soloists on the second Friday of December (Christmas Concert) and on Good Friday.

*Figure 6.30* Sanctuary Organ and Concerts page

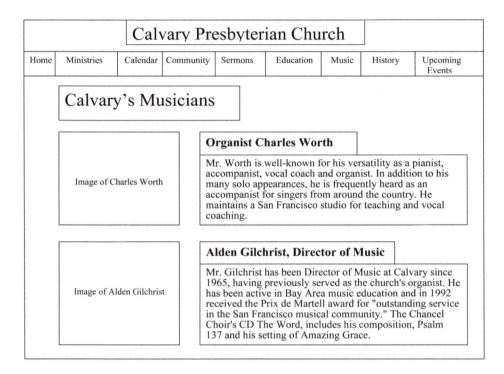

*Figure 6.31* Calvary's Musicians page

Apart from information about the three choirs, the *Calvary's Choirs* page contains the links for downloading the music samples offered on the original *Music at Calvary* page, and a mention of musical performances by all three choirs, also taken from the original page. Both these items could be incorporated in the non-linear model but it would result in an increase in complexity which we felt would clutter the original model.

As for the *Calvary's Musicians* page (Figure 6.31), we opted for placing the images in the Given position following the usual curriculum vitae convention. We chose the same solution on the *Sanctuary Organ and Concerts* page in order to keep the design consistent and because it does seem to be the correct position at least for the *Sanctuary Organ* image–text combination. The text, which we kept from the original page, describes the organ and its setting, and therefore it naturally follows the image of the organ. The situation with the *Concerts at Calvary* image–text combination is the opposite since the concerts are talked about in general and the image is a specific example. The text should thus ideally come first, but for the sake of overall consistency of design, we kept to the solution of having the image in the Given position as well.

Compared with the original design, the redesigned *Music at Calvary* page results in three additional pages at the third layer of the website structure, which may not seem very economical. However, much is gained – clarity of the exposition of content, overall consistency of design, as well as elimination of the need for scrolling. As for the clear exposition of content, we have argued that the non-linear semantics of content of any importance should best be represented explicitly, first by an appropriate non-linear model and then by its translation into different forms of layout and navigation. The *Music at Calvary* page in the original Calvary Church website contains much information and the *Music* link is included in the website's first-layer navigation bar. Both are good reasons for assuming that music is an important part of the content of the Calvary website and thus deserves to have its non-linear content made explicit in the way we have done.

The next semantic field we will deal with is *our community*. As we said, this should be a first-layer navigation link and it should be at least briefly outlined on the home page. *Our community* consists of various groups of people affiliated with the church, namely staff, various fellowships and what we will call 'friends'. In the original design, these are dispersed throughout various pages of the website. *Our community* and its three subcategories themselves are about what people are, rather than about what they do. This certainly depends on their activities to an extent, but the emphasis is on identifying the people, not the activities. The curricula on the staff page are a good example. *Fellowships*, which in the original design was on the *Ministries and Fellowships* page, will be separated from ministries on that basis, since ministries are about what people do, rather than who they are, and will be moved from the *Ministries and Fellowships* (*Calvary Activities*) page to *Our Community* page. *Friends* are people that crop up throughout the website as being somehow related to the church but without being staff members. They seem to do certain things for the church such as leading education, fellowship, ministry and other activities, and they also give sermons, but their role in relation to the church is not clearly defined. Their names and email addresses are usually mentioned at the bottom of the pages that describe the fellowships, ministries, etc.

The structure of *our community* semantic field is a simple classification tree, as in Figure 6.32.

An example of a path through the tree is presented in a second translation in Figures 6.33, 6.34 and 6.35. We chose the *Club Calvary* path as an illustration but the other paths follow the same pattern. The second translation consists of screens with covert tree navigation systems and follows our hierarchy of periodicity approach.

We will now briefly focus on redesigning the original website's *Ministries and Fellowships* (*Calvary Activities*) page. We have already taken the *Fellowships* and associated links and transformed them into a category of their own, having a second-layer navigation button. But the rest of the categorization on the *Ministries and Fellowships* (*Calvary Activities*) page also needs sorting out. First of all, we will group the different activities that are under *Education* in the original site (*Sunday morning schedule for children and youth, Young adult bible study, Lydia circle, Social witness*, etc.) together with *Adult education*. We believe that *Children's choir* should

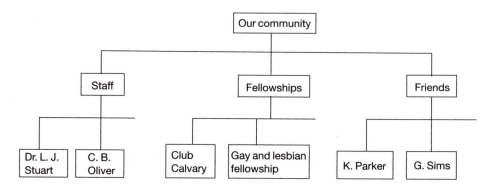

*Figure 6.32* Non-linear model of the 'community' semantic field

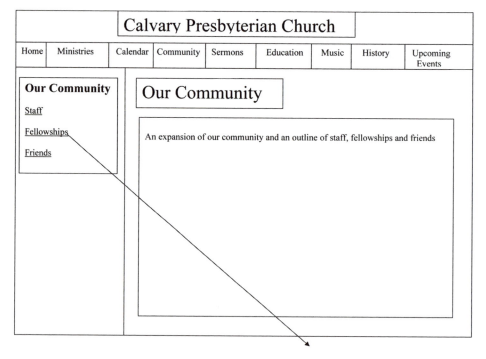

*Figure 6.33* Our Community page

be another subordinate of education, since it is about teaching children how to sing. However, the education subcategories that are presently all lumped together should be sorted into *Children and youth education*, *Adult education* and *General education*. The resulting structure of the *education* semantic field is presented in Figure 6.36 and its second translation at the second layer of website structure is in Figure 6.37.

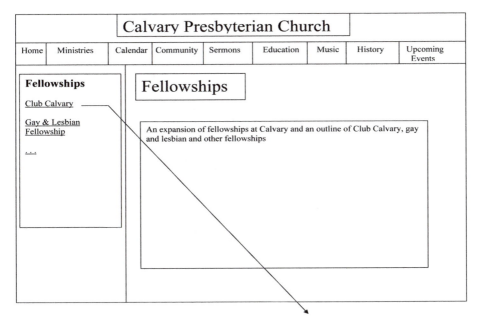

*Figure 6.34* Fellowships page

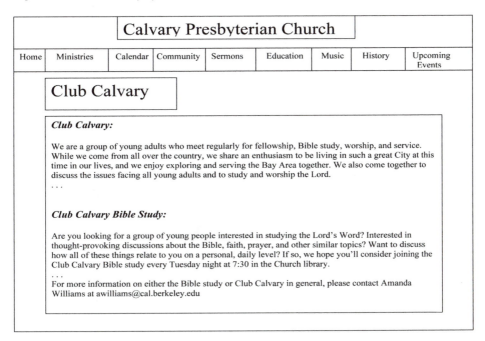

*Figure 6.35* Club Calvary page

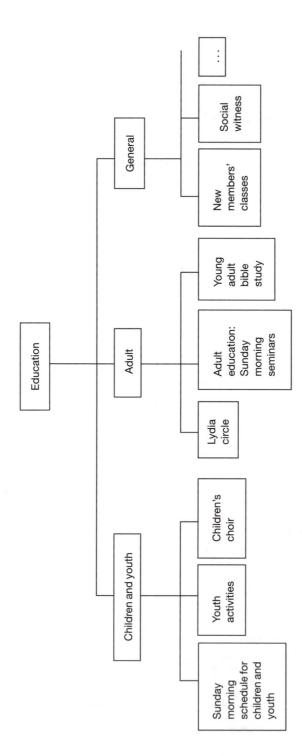

*Figure 6.36* A redesigned semantic field of 'education' on the Calvary website

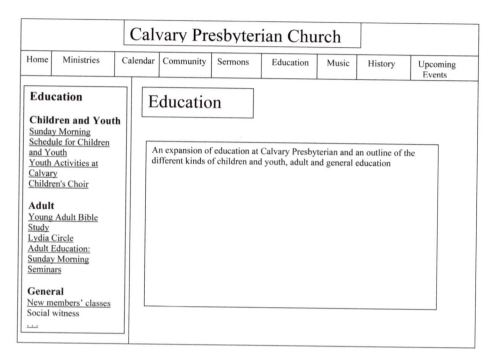

*Figure 6.37* Second translation of the semantic field of 'education'

Since there does not seem to be enough information, or even a need, for a layer of the site structure where the *children and youth, adult* and *general* kinds of education would be introduced, that layer is left out and the categories appear, instead, as non-clickable headings on the covert navigation tree. The links in the covert navigation tree lead to pages at the third layer of website structure, each page providing information about the appropriate topic.

We will finally redesign the *ministries* semantic field. Going back to the original *Ministries and Fellowships* page (Figure 6.19), it is obvious that *Baptism* and *Weddings* should not be subsumed under *Education,* since they are a kind of service and should therefore be grouped together with *Board of Deacons* under *Ministries.* Having *Music at Calvary* under *Worship* on the *Ministries and Fellowships* (*Calvary Activities*) page does not seem to make much sense either since it is neither a ministry nor a fellowship.

The reconceptualized *ministries* semantic field is thus a simple tree presented in Figure 6.38 and its second translation at the second layer of the site structure is in Figure 6.39.

The links in the covert tree navigation lead to third-layer pages that provide information about the various topics.

Our redesign of this website has, so far, followed our first and second translation

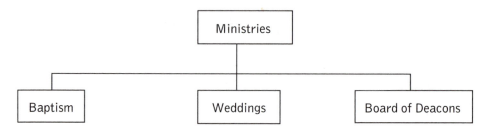

*Figure 6.38* A non-linear model of the 'ministries' semantic field

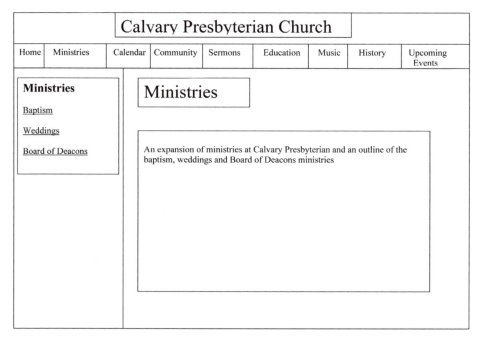

*Figure 6.39* Second translation of the 'ministries' semantic field (second layer of structure)

principles, and focused on the strategically most important semantic relations between the chunks of website content. There is just one further aspect to be dealt with – linking the various pieces of content that are dispersed throughout the website by network relations. The original website does not do this, but to navigate a site of this kind with ease, it is vitally important to achieve overall integration of content. We will again show just a few network relations to exemplify the general principle.

Two pages that lend themselves well to being linked by network relations are the *Staff* page and the *Recent Sermons* page. Most of the sermons are in fact given by staff, in particular by Dr Laird J. Stuart and Rev. Kevin Doty. A link between information about A. Gilchrist on the *Music at Calvary* page and on the *Staff* page will

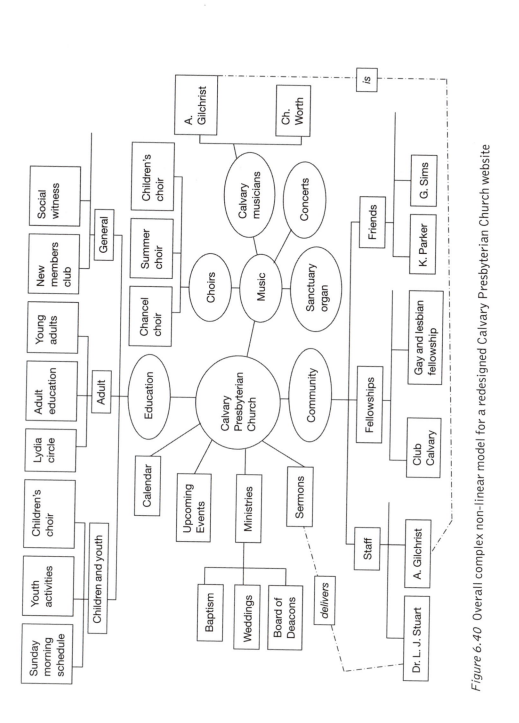

Figure 6.40 Overall complex non-linear model for a redesigned Calvary Presbyterian Church website

also help to make a clearer connection between the members of the church commu-nity and their activities. Links between the names of the community members who lead the various church activities and the staff page would perform the same function of identifying who the leaders are and would add their current activities to their curri-cula. On the other hand, Rev. Kevin Doty is said to have been called an Associate Pastor for Discipleship in his curriculum, but there is no more specific information that would enable links to be made to the various education activities he is mentioned as leading in the *Education* category.

The overall complex non-linear model that integrates all the other, more local models we have discussed in this section is shown in Figure 6.40. Only the parts we have redesigned are mapped out in detail, but the rest could easily have been rede-signed in the same way. So as not to clutter the display, only two network links are shown.

# 7 Afterword

We have presented a comprehensive theory of new media design. We have identified its basic building blocks, which are the semantic constructs that we call non-linear models and that underlie the non-linear structure of new media products. The non-linear models are what may be referred to as the new media semantics. We have specified the different ways these basic semantic components are translated into the forms of new media products (the second translation rules). We have also shown how they combine to create complex non-linear models and how these are sequenced to form new media non-linear, multimodal texts. And finally we have linked the selection of non-linear models in new media design to the goals, or strategies that designers attempt to achieve, which ultimately are (or should be) motivated by the target audience of the new media products.

We thus consider new media design to be a semiotic system consisting of meanings and forms. There is a strongly motivated relationship between the meanings and forms since we do not recognize forms that do not have particular meanings behind them. There is of course diversification between the two levels of the semiotic system, and each meaning, or non-linear model, can be expressed by a considerable variety of forms. Which form is selected in any particular instance is motivated by coding orientations, which depend on the characteristics of the target audience. We have demonstrated that our approach can be used both for designing new media products from scratch and for redesigning existing products.

We have argued that the non-linear semantics of new media products should be more closely related to their forms than has so far been the case. Our study is not just descriptive of what design already is, but proposes a new way forward. We provide a blueprint or a road map for how we believe new media design should evolve. Our argument is based on a theory of new media design as a kind of language, and we have drawn extensively on our knowledge of language and other semiotic systems when developing it. The new media are a mode of communication and a semiotic perspective on its design thus appears very appropriate. We are not aware of any approach to new media design that is, in this regard, as comprehensive and systematic as ours.

We have put a strong emphasis on the designer's strategy and purpose since we believe that the choice of non-linear models and their translations, or realizations, should be deliberate. There is of course space for creativity, and unintended consequences of one choice over another will no doubt arise. Design is, however, different from art where the depth of the unconscious may be explored and consequently a more interpretive approach may be desirable.

## Creativity

We have already discussed how metaphor can be used creatively to a considerable effect when translating non-linear models into navigation and interface (Chapter 4). But other second translations can also be seen as aesthetically motivated – apart from being pleasing for the eye, the use of images to translate relations that usually are translated by text (see, e.g., Figures 4.11 and 4.49) can be considered creative since it is a way of translating complex conceptual structures that is not yet well established in new media design. Such complex semantic fields are still typically translated by text, as they are in the old media such as print. This should not really be a surprise since text does lend itself to expressing complex logical arguments and relations, whereas images, except perhaps for diagrams, tend to be better suited to making an impression. But this is not necessarily the only way of doing things. It is also not surprising because many, perhaps most, new media designers initially trained in old media design, and then applied this to new media. It requires a certain amount of creative effort, apart from considerable visual literacy, to be able to use images the way text is usually used, and a reflexive approach to one's own practices is also needed in order not to more or less mechanically apply design solutions that worked for the old media to the new.

Much is, however, gained. Translating non-linear semantics into text usually results in implicit translations as we have seen (Figure 4.18), and the possibility of making this semantics explicit, which is best achieved by translations into image processes as well as by metaphorical translations, is lost, together with the chance of making it easier to understand for the consumer.

Some of the variations on the basic generic structure we outlined in Chapter 5 can also be seen as aesthetically motivated. There we explained the possibility of skipping a layer of structure as having a functional motivation – simply by there not being enough to say about a topic, or semantic field. But a designer can also use this variation on the basic pattern in order to make the target audience work harder to figure out what the overall semantics of the product is about, to create a kind of puzzle, in other words. This is similar to how some advertisements use jumps of logic in order to attract the viewers' attention and be more engaging and more entertaining. Just as with good advertisements, however, this semantic play cannot be gratuitous or be taken too far. There must be some system which those logical leaps refer to, and which the viewer or consumer is then invited to fill in. As Csikszentmihalyi (1997: 104) put it:

> After an insight occurs, one must check it out to see if the connections genuinely make sense. The painter steps back from the canvas to see whether the composition works, the poet rereads the verse with a more critical eye, the scientist sits down to do the calculations or run the experiments.

True creativity is only possible within the constraints of what is accepted or typical – but if the insight is right, these boundaries may be pushed and the system itself modified.

One more factor that seems to stay in the way of creative solutions to translating new media semantics is the insistence of some usability experts on using familiar metaphors, and generally familiar ways of design, in order to make new media better usable. The reasoning is that if new media adopt design conventions that are already familiar to most users from other contexts (e.g. the book table-of-contents metaphor for navigation, as discussed in Chapter 1), the new media will not require too much mental effort from the user to get past the design itself, and the user will thus be able to focus on the content, which is in any case what really matters. As should be obvious by now, we do not accept this reasoning as a matter of principle. If one follows this approach, one keeps doing things the way they have always been done, and one does not take advantage of the new media potential for a design that does not have to obey old media constraints, and that can be used to make complex non-linear semantics explicit and thus easier to understand for the user. Rather paradoxically then, from the point of view of cognitive labour, it is the new design principles, the principles that break with the old media conventions, which make new media products more usable.

## Interactivity

One aspect of new media that is usually considered rather important (see, e.g., Sims 1997, 2000), and that we have not spent much time on explicitly discussing, is inter-activity. We see interactivity as deriving from non-linearity and multimodality, and have therefore focused on writing about these. As we demonstrated in Chapter 5, a generic stage can be interpreted from the point of view of ideational and textual meaning. What we did not discuss is that, as is the case with the clause, or simple sentence, as well as with genre in linguistic texts, generic stages in new media design can also be seen interpersonally, by focusing on the way each generic stage functions as a piece of interaction.

It is true that the ideational aspect of a generic stage consists of one level of a simple non-linear model and of its second translation. It is also true that this ideational content is articulated by the textual function as an outline–condensation–expansion pattern.

But, just as in the case of the clause, the generic stage in new media design can also be seen as having an interpersonal, or interactive structure. The interpersonal aspect of the clause meaning is formed by the various functions of clause as a speech act – the different ways it expresses what the speaker wants to say and how this affects the hearer. At the lowest degree of detail, the clause will fulfil one of four fundamental speech functions: that of the statement, of giving information to the hearer; that of the question, of demanding some information from the hearer; that of the command, of asking the hearer for some goods or services; or, finally, that of the offer, of giving some goods to the hearer or performing some services for him/her by means of language (see Figure 1.2). All these speech functions are distinguished from one another by different grammatical realizations (see Halliday 1994).

Since such speech acts do not occur in isolation but are always part of an interaction, they always occur in a sequence. There are different typical sequences of them, and these are specified by exchange structure, which has been given this name because it maps out how the exchange of information or goods and services occurs (e.g. Berry 1981, O'Donnell 1990, Martin 1992).

Now, as we said before, the various parts of the generic stage in new media design can also be seen as sequences of speech acts, or speech functions, which make up an exchange structure. The outline of the next layer of a product's structure can be interpreted as *cueing* the user, as presenting a teaser of what is to follow – some information, although not much, is given. This component of the generic stage is most often realized by statements. The cue is confirmed, or consolidated, by the presence of related navigation buttons – the information in the cue is re-presented, or *consolidated*, in a condensed form. This consolidation is often realized by short statements again, or even short statements followed by commands – e.g. when rolled over, the image of one of the guns functioning as navigation buttons in Figure 5.7 changes to *arquebus* (an implicit statement – 'this is arquebus') and *click for more information* (a command).

Upon seeing the navigation buttons, the user clicks on the one that s/he is interested in. By doing so, s/he gives a command to the computer – s/he requests a service, namely s/he *demands* the computer to take him/her to the relevant page at the next layer of structure. Finally, upon landing on the requested page, the computer gives the user more information – it expands, or *amplifies*, the information given earlier in the outline and navigation buttons, and this is usually realized by statements again. And so this exchange structure goes on iteratively, until the user obtains all the information s/he is interested in.

There are of course variations on the basic pattern. As we already said when talking about the ideational and textual aspects of the generic stage, the outline, or 'cue', can be left out. It can also be realized not by statements, but for instance by commands, as in 'We want you to learn how to construct your website so that you can raise the maximum amount of money in the shortest possible time. To find out more, click on the navigation button on the right', or by questions, as in 'Are you interested in raising money online? Do you know what it takes? . . . For advice, click on the navigation button below.' And it can even be realized by offers – 'How would you feel if we advised you on the best way of raising money online? We are going to do just that.'

The user's command can of course also be realized differently than by a mouse click, depending on the kind of interface the computer is equipped with – it can be done linguistically in the case of a voice interface, by pointing when the interface is based on touch, and so on. And the page where the information is presented in detail can consist, not just of statements, but of other speech functions as well.

How would our exchange structure apply to some of the more creative translations of the non-linear models? Let us have a look at a second translation of the 'Art Deco watches' text that makes extensive use of images to translate content which more typically would be translated by text (see Figures 4.19, 4.20 and 4.49). The introduction to the main part of the product, including the red-ink images of watches rising to form the main navigation bar (Figures 4.19 and 4.20), can be said to function as a cue to the content that follows, and the navigation buttons function as a consolidation of this cue or outline. The cue is realized by illustrated statements about how the context of the 1920s lead to developments in the watchmaking industry. The navigation buttons made up of images (e.g. the wristwatch) may be considered consolidations realized by implicit statements ('this is the wristwatch'), like in the above 'arquebus' example. The user's click on one of the navigation buttons is a command, and the subsequent appearance of the analytical process of a watch realizes an amplification of the preceding content (Figure 4.49). In terms of speech function, it is an implicit statement again – 'these are the components of the wristwatch'. The menu of the attribute types in the top-right corner of the image realizes the consolidation of the image content, and rolling over an attribute type constitutes another user's command. The appearance of the specific attributes that follow realizes an amplification of these condensed attributes. Finally, rolling over one of these specific attributes forms another command and results in its amplification in the form of labels on the relevant parts of the watch in the image.

Another interesting case is the metaphorical translation of the 'Art Deco watches' text by a narrative scenario (see Figures 4.15, 4.16 and 4.17). The introduction that sets up the scenario for the piece cues users to what will follow, after which they give a command by clicking on the *Enter* button. The first scene of the real narrative then appears, the interior of a Parisian café populated by 1920s celebrities. This forms the beginning of another exchange: most of the characters are gazing at the user and so demand (Kress and van Leeuwen 2007), or *cue*, interaction. The user clicks on one of them and so gives him/her a command, and the character complies by coming forward in a rather literal amplification of him/herself.

A dialogue box then appears and a dialogue begins which consists of several exchanges. These exchanges are quite similar to those in real-life interactions: the user initiates the first exchange by typing in a greeting and the character responds – in the example we showed in Chapter 4, Al Capone says: 'Hey man . . . wassup?' The next exchange begins by the user asking something, e.g. 'Got a light?' and closes with Capone's 'Sure buddy! So long as you ain't with that damned gendarmerie.' Capone then initiates the following exchange by pulling out a lighter-watch below which a description of its attributes pops up. The user closes this exchange by holding up his/her cigarette and lighting it – this last move, or act, is implied, or imaginary. The user then initiates a final exchange by typing in something like 'Nice lighter', to which Capone answers: 'Sure is . . . and it also lets you know you've lived to see another day.' The interaction is now finished and Capone recedes into the background again, clearing the stage for another interaction with another character that will follow the same pattern.

## Future directions

Much remains to be done. It would be interesting to carry out tests with intended target audiences to see how the usability of new media products based on our model compares with other products that follow the usual information architecture approach. It would also be interesting to test our hypothesis that following our principles of semiotic design results in a better understanding of content on the part of the target audience than is achieved by design that is less semantically motivated. We have provided a model whose advantage is that it is based on a coherent theory and we hope that, among other things, it may inspire related empirical research.

# References

Adams, S. (1995) *Always Postpone Meetings with Time-Wasting Morons*, London, Boxtree.

Aristotle (1954) *The Rhetoric and the Poetics*, New York, Random House.

Belch, G.E. and M.A. Belch (2007) *Advertising and Promotion: An Integrated Marketing Communications Perspective*, seventh edition, New York, McGraw-Hill Irwin.

Bernstein, B. (1981) 'Codes, modalities and the process of cultural reproduction: a model', *Language and Society* 10: 327–63.

Berry, M. (1981) 'Systemic linguistics and discourse analysis: a multilayered approach to exchange structure', in M.C. Coulthard and M. Montgomery (eds), *Studies in Discourse Analysis*, London, Routledge & Kegan Paul.

Bolter, J.D. and R. Grusin (2000) *Remediation: Understanding New Media*, Cambridge, MA, MIT Press.

Cagan, J. and C.M. Vogel (2000) *Creating Breakthrough Products*, Upper Saddle River, NJ, Prentice Hall.

Comenius (1658) *Orbis Sensualium Pictus*, Nurenberg.

Cooper, J.C. (1993) *An Illustrated Encyclopedia of Traditional Symbols*, London, Thames and Hudson.

Crystal, D. (1997) *The Cambridge Encyclopedia of Language*, second edition, Cambridge, Cambridge University Press.

Csikszentmihalyi, M. (1997) *Creativity: Flow and the Psychology of Discovery and Invention*, New York, HarperCollins.

de Beaugrande, R. (1980) *Text, Discourse and Process: Towards a Multidisciplinary Science of Texts*, Norwood, NJ, Ablex.

Eco, U. (1992) *Interpretation and Overinterpretation*, Cambridge, Cambridge University Press.

Eggins, S. (1994) *An Introduction to Systemic-Functional Linguistics*, London, Pinter.

Fellbaum, C. (1998) *WordNet: An Electronic Lexical Database*, Cambridge, MA, MIT Press.

Forceville, C. (1996) *Pictorial Metaphor in Advertising*, London, Routledge.

Fries, P.H. (1981) 'On the status of theme in English: arguments from discourse', *Forum Linguisticum* 6(1): 1–38.

Giddens, A. (1996) *The Nation State and Violence*, Cambridge, Polity Press.

Godin, S. (2005) *Knock, Knock: Seth Godin's Incomplete Guide to Building a Website that Works*, Do You Zoom, Inc. Available from: http://sethgodin.typepad.com

Gomez-Perez, A. and V.R. Benjamins (eds) (2002) *Knowledge Engineering and Knowledge Management: Ontologies and the Semantic Web*, Berlin, Springer.

Halliday, M.A.K. (1979) 'Modes of meaning and modes of expression: types of grammatical structure and their determination by different semantic functions', in D.J. Allerton, E. Carney and D. Holcroft (eds), *Function and Context in Linguistic Analysis: Essays Offered to William Haas*, Cambridge, Cambridge University Press.

—— (1994) *An Introduction to Functional Grammar*, second edition, London, Arnold.

Hanson, W. (2001) *Principles of Internet Marketing*, Cincinnati, South-Western College Publishing.

Harman, A. and W. Mellers (1980) *Man and His Music*, London, Barrie and Jenkins.

Jussim, E. (1983) *Visual Communication and the Graphic Arts*, New York, R.R. Bowker Co.

Kress, G. and T. van Leeuwen (2007) *Reading Images: The Grammar of Visual Design,* second edition, London, Routledge.

Lakoff, G. (1990) *Women, Fire and Dangerous Things: What Categories Reveal about the Mind*, London, University of Chicago Press.

Lakoff, G. and M. Johnson (1980) *Metaphors We Live By*, Chicago, University of Chicago Press.

Lehman, F. (ed.) (1992) *Semantic Networks in Artificial Intelligence*, Oxford, Pergamon Press.

Martin, J.R. (1991) 'Intrinsic functionality: implications for a contextual theory', *Social Semiotics* 1(1): 99–162.

—— (1992) *English Text*, Amsterdam, Benjamins.

—— (1993a) 'Technicality and abstraction: language for the creation of specialized texts', in M.A.K. Halliday and J.R. Martin (eds) *Writing Science: Literacy as Discursive Power*, London, Falmer.

—— (1993b) 'Life as a noun: arresting the universe in science and humanities', in M.A.K. Halliday and J.R. Martin (eds) *Writing Science: Literacy as Discursive Power*, London, Falmer.

Martinec, R. (2002) 'Rhythmic hierarchy in monologue and dialogue', *Functions of Language* 9(1): 39–59.

Martinec, R. and A. Salway (2005) 'A system for image–text relations in new (and old) media', *Visual Communication* 4(3): 337–71.

Neuenschwander, B. (1993) *Letterwork – Creative Letterforms in Graphic Design*, London, Phaidon.

Nielsen, J. (2000) *Designing Web Usability: The Practice of Simplicity*, Indianapolis, New Riders.

Norman, D.A. (1990) *The Design of Everyday Things*, New York, Doubleday.

O'Donnell, M. (1990) 'A dynamic model of exchange', *Word* 3: 293–328.

—— (2000) 'Intermixing multiple discourse strategies for automatic text composition', *Revista Canaria de Estudios Ingleses* 40: 115–33.

Rachowiecki, R. (1999) *Southwest*, Footscray, Vic., Lonely Planet Publications.

Raimondo Souto, M. (1967) *The Technique of the Motion Picture Camera*, London, Focal Press.

Raulet, S. (1985) *Art Deco Jewelry*, New York, Rizzoli.

Roget, H. (1966) *Roget's Thesaurus*, new edition, Harmondsworth, Penguin Books.

Roth, W.-M., L. Pozzer-Ardenghi and J. Young Han (2005) *Critical Graphicacy – Understanding Visual Representation Practices in School Science*, Dordrecht, Springer.

Schneiderman, B. (1998) *Designing the Human–Computer Interface: Strategies for Effective Human–Computer Interaction*, New York, Addison-Wesley.

Sims, R. (1997) 'Interactivity: a forgotten art?', *Computers in Human Behaviour* 13(2): 157–80.

—— (2000) 'An interactive conundrum: constructs of interactivity and learning theory', *Australian Journal of Educational Technology* 16(1): 45–57.

Sowa, J.F. (1983) *Conceptual Structures: Information Processing in Mind and Machine*, Lebanon, IN, Addison-Wesley.

Spence, R. (2001) *Information Visualization*, Boston, Addison-Wesley.

Talbot, W.H.F. (1969 [1844]) *The Pencil of Nature*, New York, Reprint.

Thibault, P. (1987) 'An interview with Michael Halliday', in R. Steele and T. Threadgold (eds), *Language Topics: Essays in Honour of Michael Halliday*, Vol. 2, Amsterdam, Benjamins.

Trachtenberg, A. (1980) *Classic Essays in Photography*. New Haven, CT, Leete's Island Books.

Tufte, E.R. (1990) *Envisioning Information*, Cheshire, CT, Graphics Press.

van Leeuwen, T. (2005) *Introducing Social Semiotics*, London, Routledge.

Veen, J. (2001) *The Art and Science of Web Design*, Indianapolis, New Riders.

Wignell, P., S. Eggins and J.R. Martin (1989) 'The discourse of geography: ordering and explaining the experiential world', *Linguistics and Education* 1(4): 359–92.

Wright, W. (1975) *Sixguns and Society: A Structural Study of the Western*, Berkeley, CA, University of California Press.

# Index

**Related titles from Routledge**

# Reading Images:
# The Grammar of Visual Design

Second Edition

## Gunther Kress and Theo van Leeuwen

Praise for the first edition:

'*Reading Images* is the most important book in visual communication since Jacques Bertin's *Semiology of Information Graphics*. It is both thorough and thought-provoking; a remarkable breakthrough.'

Kevin G. Barnhurst, *Syracuse University, USA*

This second edition of the landmark textbook *Reading Images* builds on its reputation as the first systematic and comprehensive account of the grammar of visual design. Drawing on an enormous range of examples from children's drawings to textbook illustrations, photo-journalism to fine art, as well as three-dimensional forms such as sculpture and toys, the authors examine the ways in which images communicate meaning.

Features of this fully updated second edition include:

- new material on moving images and on colour
- a discussion of how images and their uses have changed through time
- websites and web-based images
- ideas on the future of visual communication.

*Reading Images* focuses on the structures or 'grammar' of visual design – colour, perspective, framing and composition – providing the reader with an invaluable 'tool-kit' for reading images and making it a must for anyone interested in communication, the media and the arts.

ISBN13: 978–0–415–31914–0 (hbk)
ISBN13: 978–0–415–31915–7 (pbk)
ISBN13: 978–0–203–61972–8 (ebk)

**Available at all good bookshops**
**For ordering and further information please visit:**
**www.routledge.com**